*To my
former dormmates — warm friends
and fellow ministers*

Bob Barrett
Dale Fisher
Jim Grier
Tom Manley
Don Messenger
Fred Patton

Contents

Photos

Maps

Preface

"Do you understand what you are reading?" That question was asked by the deacon-evangelist Philip of the Ethiopian eunuch in the wilderness near Gaza (Acts 8:30). This answer was given: "How can I, except some man should guide me?" (Acts 8:31). Only the Spirit of God can open the spiritual understanding of a man to perceive the truth of the written Word of God, but the Spirit has also chosen to perform that task through appointed preachers and teachers. God can teach us directly from His Word and He can also teach us through what He has taught others.

This commentary has been designed to teach the Word of God to others. It is an attempt to make clear the meaning of the English text (King James Version) through organization, exposition, and careful usage of the Greek text. It is planned as a readable commentary with nontechnical vocabulary and smooth transition from one section to another. It has been divided into thirteen chapters so that it could be used by adult Sunday school classes or Bible study groups for a traditional quarter of thirteen weeks. It could very easily be adapted into a six-month study by devoting two sessions to each chapter. At the end of each chapter are found discussion questions, designed to stimulate personal study and to make relevant the truth of God. The book can also be used by one person alone as a private Bible study guide. In either case, this commentary should be read with an open Bible. It is the author's prayer and hope that men and women will be blessed and edified as they undertake a study of I Corinthians with the aid of this volume.

A special word of thanks is extended to Cornelius Zylstra, editor of Baker Book House, who encouraged me to undertake this project. Also, my love and appreciation go to my dear wife, Gloria, who carefully typed the manuscript (Prov. 31:31).

Introduction

I. WRITER

Very little question is raised about the Pauline authorship of this book. Both at the beginning and end of the book, the author identified himself as Paul (1:1; 16:21). He claimed to be an apostle (1:1; 4:9; 9:1; 15:9) and to have seen the resurrected Christ (9:1; 15:8). Both of these assertions correspond to Paul's life history, recorded both by him elsewhere (Gal. 1:1, 12) and by Luke (Acts 9:1–16; 14:14). He looked upon Timothy in a spiritual father-son relationship (4:17; cf. I Tim. 1:2). He used himself and Apollos, both prominent in the establishment of the Corinthian church, as illustrations of the functions of ministers (1:12; 3:4–5; 4:6; cf. Acts 18:24–28). Finally, he disclosed that he had preached in Corinth (2:1–5) and that he had laid the foundation of the church (3:10). This could only refer to Paul's visit to Corinth during his second missionary journey (Acts 18:1–18). All of these points, added up together, make a strong case for Pauline authorship.

II. CITY OF CORINTH

Corinth was located on a narrow strip of land, called an isthmus, connecting the Peloponnesus with northern Greece. This isthmus also formed the land bridge between the Aegean and the Adriatic seas. Located forty miles west of Athens, Corinth was the capital of this southern province called Achaia. The Romans had destroyed the city in 146 B.C., but because its location was so important, they later rebuilt it under Julius Caesar in 46 B.C. By the time Paul arrived in the city (A.D.

50-52), the city had grown to a population of 500,000. Today only the ruins of the city remain.

In that day Corinth was the crossroads for travel and commerce, both north and south for the Greek peninsula and east and west from Rome to the Near East. It had two seaports, Cenchrea on the Aegean Sea to the east and Lechaeum on the edge of the Gulf of Corinth to the west. Commercial ships, instead of sailing around the dangerous southern tip of Greece, were portaged across the isthmus from one port to the other. This saved time and was less risky. Thus Corinth became a city of wealth and pleasure. People went there with money to spend and to indulge themselves in varied pleasures.

On the highest point in the city stood the pagan temple of Aphrodite, the goddess of love, full of religious prostitutes to serve the wishes of its devotees. These women also participated in the night life of the city. Also located at Corinth was a stadium where athletic contests, next best to the Greek Olympics, were held every two years. Although Corinth was influenced by the

The Corinth Canal, near the site of ancient Corinth. The canal, completed in 1893, was partially excavated in Roman times, under Nero, with forced labor including Jewish captives.

philosophy of Athens it never became a center of intellectual learning. The citizens and the tourists were too busy making and spending money to do much rationalistic speculation. Because it was a mercantile center, all kinds of people settled there: Romans, Greeks, and Jews. Corinth became a cosmopolitan city with all of the attending vices attached to that type of society.

III. ESTABLISHMENT OF THE CHURCH

The founding of the Corinthian church was recorded by Luke in Acts (18:1–18). From Athens Paul had sent his associates Silas and Timothy back to the Macedonian churches at Philippi, Thessalonica, and Berea (Acts 17:15–16; cf. I Thess. 3:1–6), which were started earlier on this same (second) missionary journey. When Paul therefore left Athens for Corinth, he went alone. Cut off from his friends and supporting churches, Paul worked at tentmaking, a craft he had learned as a youth (Acts 18:3), to meet his financial needs. He found both work and lodging with a Jewish couple, Aquila and Priscilla, who practiced this same craft and who had been expelled from Rome because of the anti-Semitic decree of Caesar Claudius. Perhaps through personal conversation with Paul and his subsequent synagogue preaching, this couple came to know Jesus Christ as their Messiah and Savior.

During the week, Paul worked with his hands, but every Sabbath he was in the synagogue, logically proving from the Old Testament that the promised Messiah had to suffer death and be raised from the dead, and that Jesus was indeed that promised Savior (cf. Acts 17:2–3). Many in attendance, both Jews and Gentile proselytes to the Jewish religion, were convinced and believed. When Silas and Timothy joined Paul at Corinth with a good report of the faith and stedfastness of the Macedonian Christians, Paul was constrained to press the claims of Jesus Christ even more strongly upon his synagogue listeners. When this occurred, the Jews resisted and blasphemed, forcing Paul to leave the synagogue with this declaration: "Your blood be upon your own heads; I am clean: from henceforth I will go unto the Gentiles" (18:6). It was also about this time that Paul wrote I Thessalonians, based upon the content of Timothy's report.

Paul then moved his ministry into the house of Justus, which

Paul's Second Missionary Journey

was adjacent to the Jewish synagogue. Soon after, the chief ruler of the synagogue, Crispus, along with his family, believed. From this new site, a ministry to the pagan, idolatrous Corinthians was begun with much success. The opposition must have been intense at that time because Paul received special encouragement from God. He was informed that he would not suffer bodily harm and that many would be converted through his ministry. Paul then labored for eighteen months (A.D. 50-52) both as an evangelist and as a teacher of the new congregation.

In the midst of his ministry at Corinth, the Jews brought charges against Paul before Gallio, the political deputy or proconsul of Achaia (Acts 18:12–17). Since the accusations were religious and not political in nature, Gallio refused to arbitrate the matter. In driving the Jews from the judgment seat, Gallio declared the innocence of Paul and recognized the troublesome character of the Jews. Later, the Gentile proselytes to Judaism beat Sosthenes, the chief ruler of the synagogue, who probably was a Gentile himself and a recent convert to Christianity; again, Gallio reacted negatively.

Even after this burst of persecution, Paul remained a "good while" in Corinth. With Aquila and Priscilla he then left Corinth and set sail for Antioch in Syria via Ephesus.

IV. TIME AND PLACE

Paul left Aquila and Priscilla at Ephesus and sailed for Caesarea (Acts 18:18–22). On his arrival he visited the Jerusalem church and then returned to his home church at Antioch. After spending "some time there, he departed, and went over all the country of Galatia and Phrygia in order, strengthening all the disciples" (18:23). Thus began his third missionary journey. During this period of Paul's absence from Ephesus, Apollos, an eloquent Jewish teacher of the doctrine of John the Baptist, came to that city and was led to a knowledge of Christ by Aquila and Priscilla. With his new faith Apollos traveled to Corinth in Achaia where he was received by the Corinthian believers and where he had a successful public ministry among the Jews (Acts 18:24–28).

A relief of the seven-branched candlestick, from a synagogue of New Testament times.

While Apollos was in Corinth, Paul reached Ephesus where he ministered for the next three years (A.D. 52-55; Acts 19:1–10; 20:31). About this time, because of increasing factionalism in the Corinthian church, Apollos left that city and returned to Ephesus (I Cor. 1:12; 16:12). Some have suggested that Paul made a quick, personal visit to Corinth to arbitrate the controversy but was unsuccessful (II Cor. 2:1; 12:14). Although this cannot be documented, it may have taken place. Since Corinth was only two hundred miles west across the Aegean Sea from Ephesus, travel and communication between the two cities was comparatively easy.

The situation at Corinth continued to deteriorate. Members of the household of Chloe brought Paul a firsthand report of the divisions within the assembly (I Cor. 1:11). They were followed by three members of the Corinthian church (Stephanas, Fortunatus, and Achaicus) who brought Paul a financial gift (16:17). Perhaps they also carried to Paul a letter from the church in which questions were asked about various doctrinal and moral issues (7:1). Thus, through personal conversations with Apollos, the Chloe household, and the three church emissaries, plus the content of the letter, Paul learned about the troubled state of the Corinthian church. Unable to leave Ephesus at that time (16:3–9), Paul did the next best thing; he wrote this letter to resolve the many problems. It was probably written near the end of his ministry at Ephesus, for he states that he had already made plans for leaving the province of Asia (16:5–7). Thus, it is reasonable to assume that it was composed during the fall or winter of A.D. 55, because he said that he would stay at Ephesus until Pentecost (16:8).

Who took the letter from Paul to Corinth? It is difficult to be positive here. Some speculation has centered around Timothy; but would Paul have written "now if Timotheus come" (16:10) if he had planned to send the letter by him? Timothy did leave Ephesus for Macedonia (Acts 19:22), probably before Paul wrote the letter. It may be that Paul was informing the Corinthian church that Timothy might visit it after his ministry in Macedonia was over. Paul did want to send Apollos back to Corinth, but Apollos refused to go (16:12). It may be that the return of the three church members (Stephanus, Fortunatus, and Achaicus) afforded Paul the chance to send the epistle back with them (16:12; cf. 16:17–18). This latter view seems to be the most plausible.

V. PURPOSES

The purposes for writing the letter are very clear. First, Paul wanted to correct the problems mentioned to him in the personal reports (chaps. 1 — 6). He rebuked the existence of church factions and tried to bring unity out of division (1:10 — 4:21). He then attempted to discipline in absentia the fornicators in their midst (5:1–13). Apparently, all visitors to Paul from Corinth brought news of this incest. He also tried to prevent warring church members from going to civil court against each other (6:1–8). To those who abused themselves sexually, he taught the sanctity of the believer's body (6:9–20).

Second, the rest of the book deals with the questions raised in the letter which Paul received from the church at Corinth: "Now concerning the things whereof ye wrote unto me" (7:1). With that letter probably before him, Paul logically moved from one issue to another. He marked his movement and change of subject with the key introductory word "Now" (see 7:1, 25; 8:1; 11:2, 17; 12:1; 15:12; 16:1). In this part of his letter Paul answered their questions concerning the necessity and the problems of marriage (7:1–24); the status of virgins and widows (7:25–40), the application of Christian liberty to the eating of meat sacrificed to idols (8:1 — 11:1), the conduct of women in the church (11:2–16), the order of the communion service (11:17–34), the nature and use of spiritual gifts — especially those of speaking in tongues and prophecy (12:1 — 14:40), the necessity and nature of the resurrection body (15:1–58), and the financial collection for the poor saints at Jerusalem (16:1–4).

In addition, he wanted to announce to them his plans to visit Corinth after a tour of the Macedonian churches (16:5–18). He then closed by extending greetings to them from the Asian churches and brethren (16:19–24).

VI. LOST LETTER

In 5:9 Paul penned, "I wrote unto you in an epistle not to company with fornicators." Does this statement mean that Paul had sent a short letter to the Corinthian church before his composition of this First Epistle? If so, what happened to it and what did it contain? Was it an inspired letter or simply human correspondence? These are difficult questions with no easy answers, but there are two plausible alternatives.

If Paul did write a previous letter, its theme was the relationship of Christians to fornicators. Apparently the Corinthians misunderstood Paul's teaching and thought that they should be separate from all immoral men. However, in this section (5:1–13) Paul corrected that notion by calling for separation only from professing believers who practiced fornication or other public sins; he did not mean that they should dissociate themselves from the unsaved fornicators. If Paul did send a previous letter, the content of the original letter was summarized and incorporated into this section (5:1–13); in which case, the church is not lacking any inscripturated book or truth. This "lost letter" may also have included Paul's plans for a return visit to Corinth (cf. II Cor. 1:15–16) and instructions for the Corinthians' part in the collection for the Jerusalem saints (II Cor. 8:6, 10; 9:1–2).

If this letter did exist and became lost, such a situation is by no means unique. After the council at Jerusalem was over, the church leaders wrote letters to the Gentile churches informing the latter of their decisions (Acts 15:20, 23–27); none of these letters has ever been found. However, the content of those letters was incorporated into Luke's record of those proceedings. The letter that the Corinthians wrote to Paul (7:1) is also lost, but the content of that letter is revealed in the answers given by Paul (7:1 — 16:4).

The second alternative is that 5:9 does not refer to a former letter, but to the epistle Paul was presently writing. The Greek verb translated "wrote" (*egrapsa*) can be interpreted to mean that Paul looked at his present discussion of fornication from the viewpoint of the Corinthian readers. At the time they would read Paul's admonition, his writing of it would be in the past. This is why he used a past verbal tense ("wrote") rather than the present ("write"). It is difficult to be positive here, but either alternative is an acceptable evangelical option.

Some of those who accept the thesis of a lost letter actually believe that parts of this lost letter can be seen in both epistles

(I Cor. 6:12-20; II Cor. 6:14 — 7:1). However, this theory rests merely upon subjective speculation, not upon objective external or textual evidence for its support. The first passage deals with the believer's relationship to his own body, and the second warns against involvement with unbelievers rather than against involvement with professing believers who are guilty of sexual sins. They treat subjects other than those in the passage under discussion (5:1–13).

The Correction of Church Division

I Corinthians 1

The church at Corinth was riddled with problems. Where should Paul start in his attempt to bring order out of chaos? The letter of inquiry sent from the church to the apostle could have provided a logical starting point, but issues raised in the letter, although important in themselves, were only symptomatic of a deeper problem. Paul knew that he had to deal with the real cause of the Corinthian dilemma, not just with its effects. This is why he devoted the first four chapters to a diagnosis and a treatment of the main spiritual disease of the church: carnality manifested in contentions.

I. BASIS OF CORRECTION (1:1–9)

The first nine verses include the usual opening remarks of a typical first-century Greek letter or epistle: author, addressee, and greeting. However, Paul's introduction is more extensive and contains a distinctively Christian feature — a prayer of thanksgiving. Also, Paul's preliminary points of courtesy are not unrelated to the main body of the letter, especially to his discussion of the first problem of church schisms. They actually reveal the kinship of the apostle to the church and the relationship of the Corinthians to the Lord Jesus Christ. These two links, therefore, form a foundation for Paul's corrective discipline.

A. Author (1:1)

Paul immediately established his authoritative position before the church by making a threefold claim for himself. He first asserted that he was an apostle.[1] Apostles were believers who had seen the resurrected Christ and who had been commissioned directly by Him to preach and to lay the foundation for the church age. Their ministries were marked by miraculous authentication and by the obedience of genuine, spiritual Christians. Throughout the Corinthian correspondence, this ring of authority can be detected in Paul's words (1:17; 2:13; 3:10; 4:9, 18–21; 5:4; 7:10; 9:1–6; 11:1; 12:28; 15:8–10; II Cor. 1:1; 12:12). Second, Paul was a called apostle.[2] He did not assume the position as did subsequent false teachers in the church (II Cor. 11:13–15), nor was he appointed by human, apostolic vote, as was Matthias (Acts 1:15–26). Paul had seen Christ in a post-ascension appearance and was directly called by Him into the office of apostle (Acts 26:12–20; Gal. 1:1, 11–16). Third, Paul claimed that his apostleship came through the agency of the will of God. It was God the Father who decreed Paul's salvation and apostleship, and it was Christ who secured that purpose when He confronted the unbelieving Saul on the road to Damascus (Acts 9:1-16).

Paul included the name of Sosthenes as his associate in the writing of the epistle. Some have identified him as a member of the house of Chloe (cf. 1:11), but more than likely he is the chief ruler of the synagogue in Corinth who was beaten by the Greeks before Gallio's judgment seat (Acts 18:17).[3] His mention does not mean that Sosthenes was a Spirit-directed co-author with Paul; rather, Sosthenes was in total agreement with Paul's inspired counsel. This fact takes on added significance when one

---

[1]The Greek word *apostolos,* translated "apostle," comes from the verb *apostellō,* which means "to send away with a commission to do something." The original twelve apostles were selected from among many disciples to be with Christ and to be sent forth by Him to preach, heal, and cast out demons within Israel (Matt. 10:5–8; Mark 3:13–15). Excluding Judas Iscariot, the group was later recommissioned by the resurrected Christ to preach the gospel throughout the world (Matt. 28:16–20).

[2]The phrase "called apostle" literally translates *klētos apostolos.* The infinitive "to be" is in italics because it is not found in the Greek text. The word "called" is an adjective, not a verb.

[3]The name "Sosthenes" is found in only two New Testament passages (Acts 18:17; I Cor. 1:1).

Temple of Apollo at Corinth. Erected in 590 B.C., the structure was an impressive tourist attraction even in New Testament times.

realizes that Sosthenes doubtless became a Christian after his beating, belonged to the Corinthian church, and knew many of the parties who were at variance with each other. Paul described him as "the brother," a spiritual brother both to Paul and to the Corinthians. Some have seen Sosthenes as Paul's secretary or amanuensis, but this position lacks solid support.[4]

B. Readers (1:2)

In his epistles, Paul exhorted believers about proper behavior only after he explained the wealth of their spiritual position in Christ (Rom. 12:1; Eph. 4:1). Thus, Paul wanted the Corinthians to see who they were before he criticized them for their faulty deportment. He described them in six ways. First, he called them "the church of God." They were members of the one true church which Christ built and purchased through His redemptive death and resurrection (Matt. 16:18; Acts 20:28; Eph.

[4]The amanuensis of Romans was Tertius (Rom. 16:22). He is mentioned at the end of the book, not in the opening greeting.

5:25). The church, as the mystical body of Christ, has an organic unity which cannot be divided by warring, imperfect members (12:12; cf. John 17:21; Eph. 4:4–6).[5] Second, he located them at Corinth.

Third, they were sanctified positionally in Christ. The phrase, "to them that are sanctified," is the translation of one Greek word *hēgiasmenois*. Grammatically, it means that they had been sanctified or set apart by God from the world for Himself in a decisive event in the past and that they were remaining and would continue to remain in a sanctified position or standing.[6] Such a position was only possible because they were judicially accepted in the beloved Christ (Eph. 1:6).

Fourth, he designated them as "called saints." Just as Paul was an apostle by divine calling, they were saints by that same calling. Sainthood was not part of their future destiny, a goal that might not be realized because of their sin; rather, it expressed their present standing.[7] The big problem was that they were not saintly in their practice, although they had experienced the effectual call of God who was working out His sovereign purpose in their lives (Rom. 8:28–30).

Fifth, they shared the same position as believers in every place. How does one become a saint? By calling upon the name of Christ. The Corinthians had done this, and so had believers in other localities. In fact, this is the simplest definition of the pro-

---

[5]The Greek word for "church" (*ekklēsia*) is used in four different ways: (1) It referred to a secular assembly, the freemen of Ephesus, gathered together for civil business (Acts 19:32, 39, 41). (2) Stephen equated Israel in her wilderness wanderings with a church (Acts 7:38). (3) The local church was a group of believers meeting in a specific locality (Rom. 16:5). (4) The universal church includes all believers from the descent of the Holy Spirit to the return of Christ for His own.

[6]The word "sanctify" applies to four different stages of the believer's salvation. It refers to the ministry of the Holy Spirit in the person's life before conversion (Gal. 1:15; II Thess. 2:13); the time of regeneration (1:2; 6:11; cf. Heb. 10:14); the present cleansing and edifying ministry of the Christian by the Spirit through the Word of God (John 17:17); and the total separation from the effects of sin when the believer receives the incorruptible, immortal body (Eph. 5:26–27).

[7]The verb "to be" is not in the original text. The word order and usage for Paul, *klētos apostolos,* is the same for them, *klētois hagiois.*

4

cedure to secure personal salvation (Acts 2:21; 9:14, 21; Rom. 10:13).[8] Some take this phrase to mean that the epistle was addressed not only to the Corinthian church, but also to all Christians throughout the Roman world.[9] However, the specific problems resolved in the book refer to a definite church.

Sixth, they had the same Lord as other believers.

In these opening verses, Paul definitely emphasized the authoritative lordship of Jesus Christ over believers' lives. All nine verses refer to Him. The Corinthians needed to recognize that their divisive spirit was a sign of spiritual disobedience.

C. Blessing (1:3)

The typical Greek salutation employed the third person, but Paul conveyed a greater degree of intimacy by using the second person, "to you." The content of the blessing was twofold: grace and peace. These two words reflect Greek ("grace," *charis*) and Hebrew ("peace," *shalom*) concepts. The doctrine of grace reveals that God bestows blessings upon believers apart from any merit within them.[10] Leon Morris stated that peace is "not simply the absence of strife, but the presence of positive blessings. It is the prosperity of the whole man, especially his spiritual prosperity."[11] In spite of their carnality, the Corinthians continued to be showered with these blessings.

The source of the double blessing is from two persons within the divine Being: the Father and the Son, the Lord Jesus Christ. One preposition, "from" *(apo)*, links the Father and the Son to-

[8]This phrase also serves as a proof for the deity of Christ. The Old Testament claimed that calling upon the name of Jehovah would gain salvation (Joel 2:32). Peter applies this verse to calling upon the name of Jesus Christ (Acts 2:21). Thus, Jehovah is the same person as Jesus Christ.

[9]Charles Hodge believes that the phrase refers to Christians within the Roman province of Achaia in which Corinth was found. It is true that the second epistle was addressed to this group as well as to the Corinthian church (II Cor. 1:1). However, why did Paul not mention Achaia in the first epistle if that was his meaning? Cf. Charles Hodge, *Commentary on The First Epistle to the Corinthians*, pp. 4-5.

[10]Paul used several words built upon *charis* in this context: "thank," *eucharistō* (1:4); "grace," *chariti* (1:4); and "gift," *charismati* (1:7).

[11]Leon Morris, *The First Epistle of Paul to the Corinthians*, p. 35.

CALLED TO BE SAINTS

gether as the common source. Doubtless, these blessings are mediated to the child of God through the indwelling ministry of the Holy Spirit.

D. Prayer of Thanksgiving (1:4–9)

How could Paul be thankful for the Corinthians, especially since he knew about their petty differences and selfishness? And yet he was always thankful! Paul was sincere, not sarcastic, when he wrote those words. The church was probably surprised to read that Paul was thankful. They expected him to be angry or ashamed or disgusted.

Paul was thankful for five reasons.

1. For grace (1:4)

He first thanked God for the grace of God which *was* given to them. The verbal form (*dotheisēi*) refers back to the time of their conversion when they had received the free gift of righteousness through faith. He was thankful for their salvation. This formed the basis for his prayer.[12] Although there were problems, still they were saved people and, though carnal, their living was better than their previous pagan behavior.

2. For enrichment (1:5)

He was then thankful that "in every thing" they "are enriched by him." The use of the verb *eploutisthēte* (literally, "you were made rich") points out that their spiritual, plutocratic position began at their conversion. Whatever their abilities were, they were bestowed by God; the Corinthians did not possess them by heredity or education. The enrichment included both quantity ("in everything") and quality ("in all utterance and all knowledge"). In their communication of the truth ("utterance") and in their grasp of the truth ("knowledge"), they had been especially blessed.

3. For confirmation (1:6–7)

Third, Paul was thankful that "the testimony of Christ was confirmed" in their midst. This could be a testimony *about* Christ

[12]The word "for" is *epi*, which literally means "upon." The grace provided formed the foundation upon which the thanksgiving rested.

6

or a testimony *by* Christ. The former is more acceptable since Paul declared that he preached "Christ and him crucified" (2:1–2) when he originally evangelized the city. The verb "was confirmed" (*ebebaiōthē*) is used in the early Greek papyri for the legal sense of guarantee. Thus, God guaranteed or authenticated Paul's ministry to be true and authoritative by giving sign gifts through the apostle.[13] Paul claimed that his message was "in demonstration of the Spirit and of power" (2:4). Christ "confirmed the word of the apostles by the signs that followed" (Mark 16:20). The Book of Hebrews added that what was spoken by the Lord "was confirmed unto us by them that heard him; God also bearing them witness both with signs and wonders, and with divers miracles, and gifts of the Holy Ghost, according to his own will" (2:3–4). As Paul worked miracles and as supernatural endowments operated within them, the Corinthians knew that what Paul proclaimed was absolute truth. That recognition should cause them to respond to Paul's subsequent exposition and commands.

There was a double result (indicated by "so that") to the confirmation. First, they came "behind in no gift." The *charismati,* translated as "gift," can refer to the gift of salvation (Rom. 5:15), the gift of general blessings (Rom. 11:29), or to special abilities given by the Holy Spirit (12:4). In the context of this book, it must refer to the supernatural sign gifts which attended the infant church during the period of new revelation. The second result is that they were waiting for the return of Christ. Morris correctly observed: "The reference to the second coming of the Lord is unexpected. The connection of thought may be that the present foretaste of the Spirit turns our thoughts to the fuller experience of the last great day."[14] What saddened Paul was that the Corinthians had everything in which to do a work for Christ while they waited for Him, but they had failed to do so.

---

[13]Cf. J. Lanier Burns, "A Reemphasis on the Purpose of the Sign Gifts," *Bibliotheca Sacra* (July-September, 1975). Burns gives a convincing argument to show that the verb "confirmed" refers to a divine authentication of authoritative, inspired revelation, whether oral or written. These gifts thus ceased when new revelation ceased at the end of the canon.

[14]Morris, *Corinthians*, p. 37.

4. For preservation (1:8)

Paul was also thankful that God would confirm or guarantee the unblamable position of the Corinthians until Christ's return. The word "blameless" does not mean that the believers were without sin or blame in their practice. The epistle clearly shows their faults. Rather, it is a legal term. No charge of condemnation nor sentencing to eternal death would ever be brought against them in the court of divine justice. Literally, the word here translated "blameless" means "not called in" (*anegklētous*). It is the answer to Paul's rhetorical questions: "Who shall lay anything to the charge of God's elect? It is God that justifieth. Who is he that condemneth? It is Christ that died . . ." (Rom. 8:33–34).

The words "that ye may be" are in italics, which means that they are not in the original manuscript. Positionally, the Corinthians were already without judicial charge. Paul knew that God would preserve that blameless standing throughout their future behavior. The end refers to the completion of God's redemptive program for their lives which will be consummated in the day of Christ, the time of His return for His own. There is a slight problem with the antecedent of "who," the relative pronoun which begins the verse. It could refer to Christ, who had just been mentioned in the previous verse, or it could go back to God the Father (1:4). The latter seems more probable since the faithfulness of the Father is introduced in the next verse.

5. For faithfulness (1:9)

In the face of Corinthian unfaithfulness, Paul was thankful for God's faithfulness. God is not just true; He is also trustworthy. His word is sure and His promises are certain. His faithfulness can be seen in His sovereign call of the Corinthians to unique fellowship with other believers and with the Lord Jesus Christ in spite of God's obvious, prior knowledge of their carnal behavior subsequent to their regeneration experience. Their local fellowship was disjointed. Paul wanted them to manifest their spiritual communion with Christ in visible expressions of love within the church.

Now that the basis of correction had been established, Paul was ready to move on to their need for repentance.

II. APPEAL FOR CORRECTION (1:10–12)

In his appeal for change, Paul did not forget what he had previously written about the Corinthians. They were the church of God, sanctified, saints, and had been called into fellowship, a communion that involved even the apostle. Therefore, Paul approached them as brethren. This was a loving gesture and approach. Paul was not stern with them as he was with the Galatians: "O foolish Galatians, who hath bewitched you . . . ?" (Gal. 3:1). The mild connective, "now" (*de*, 1:10), was designed for them to see their schisms in the light of the fellowship into which they had been brought. Even his choice of verb, "beseech" (*parakalō*),[15] manifested his soft approach. Paul did not command them; rather, he exhorted or urged them. The authority for the appeal came through Christ. Paul's directives did not contain mere human counsel; rather, what he wrote was the voice of Christ telling His church what they ought to do. Disobedience to the epistle would result in divine chastisement; obedience would bring heavenly blessing.

A. Goals of the Appeal (1:10b)
1. Unity of speech

Paul hoped to achieve three goals by his appeal.[16] The first was their unity of speech. He wanted *all* to "speak the same thing." This does not mean that they should be sure to repeat the same words, but rather, that they were to mean the same thing when they spoke. Also, their attitude in speaking had to be improved. Since they had been enriched by God in gifts or oral communication (cf. 1:5), they should speak for God's glory and proclaim His truth in love (Eph. 4:15).

2. Elimination of schisms

The second goal was the elimination of schisms. The Greek word for "divisions" is *schismata*, transliterated into the English as

[15]One of the titles for the Holy Spirit is based upon this verb. He is the Comforter, or the Paraclete (John 14:16). The verb is also used in other key Pauline appeals (Rom. 12:1; Eph. 4:1).

[16]Hodge thinks that Paul had only one goal: "that ye all speak the same thing." He sees the next two phrases as explanatory of the first, giving both the negative and the positive features. Cf. Hodge, *Corinthians*, p. 12.

'schisnv." Biblical authors used it to refer to a rent garment, torn but not yet separated into two pieces (Matt. 9:16), and to the division of opinion within Israel over the person of Christ (John 7:43). The church was marked by internal strife, but it was not yet organizationally split. This can be seen in the fact that Paul wrote to all of the factions who were still within the single church. The schisms already existed (cf. 11:18). Paul wanted the schisms to be eliminated and the church to remain in a schism-free state after the problems had been resolved.

3. Unity of attitude

The final goal was the unity of mind and judgment. To accomplish this, their opposing attitudes and opinions would have to "be perfectly joined together." The verb translated "joined" (*katartizo*) was used by the pagan Greeks for the setting of broken bones and for reconciling political factions. In the New Testament, it referred to the mending of fishing nets (Matt. 4:21). The same word is translated "restore" in Paul's directive: "Brethren, if a man be overtaken in a fault, ye which are spiritual, restore such an one in the spirit of meekness, considering thyself, lest thou also be tempted" (Gal. 6:1). It is written as "perfect" when Paul wanted to "perfect that which is lacking in your faith" (I Thess. 3:10), namely the moral and doctrinal deficiencies of the young Thessalonian converts. The Greek construction of "be perfectly joined together"[17] means that Paul wanted their differences to be mended or repaired in such a way as to remain joined together permanently. The force of his appeal was "Let's get this problem solved once and for all!"

B. Reason for the appeal (1:11–12)

The reason for the appeal is introduced by the connective word "for." Paul had received a report which he regarded as fact and not rumor. Even though his information was secondhand, Paul did not question it. This can be seen in two ways. First, he used the verb "it hath been declared" (*edēlōthē*). In the Greek papyri, that word is used of official, legal evidence. Thus, Paul

---

[17]*Ēte katērtismenoi*. The first word is the present subjunctive of *eimi*, and the second is the perfect passive participle of *katartizō*. The emphasis is on the resultant state achieved by a past action of joining together.

has been given solid proof of the Corinthian divisive spirit which doubtless was confirmed by the church messengers (16:17). Second, Paul accepted the integrity of Chloe's household. The Greek phrase literally reads, "by the ones who belong to or are related to Chloe." This could refer to her slaves, to her children, or to both. Paul would never have mentioned Chloe or her house if the evidence had not been clear and substantial. Although her Biblical identity is unknown, Chloe must have been well known to both the apostle and the church.[18]

The report declared that there were "contentions" (*erides*) within the church. This word means more than just a difference of opinion; it connotes quarrels or wranglings. It is one of the works of sinful flesh, translated as "variance" (Gal. 5:20). Written as "debate" (Rom. 1:29), it was one of the marks of the unsaved rejectors of the truth of God's creation. False teachers are characterized by it ("strife"; cf. I Tim. 6:4). The contentions, therefore, were not quiet and subtle; they had progressed to a shouting, hot-temper stage. The believers were acting and talking like unsaved men (cf. 3:3), not like saints within the church of God.

Paul then moved from the general to the specific. The phrase, "Now this I say," has the contemporary meaning, "This is what I mean." The contentions were over personalities, not over principles. It appears as if all of the Corinthians were involved in this sin (cf. "every one of you"). The church members had taken sides, following one human leader to the neglect of others. Who were these leaders? Paul cited four: Paul, Apollos, Cephas (or Peter), and Christ. Certainly these four would not have condoned this party spirit which was contrary to the spiritual oneness within Christ.

How, then, did such groups develop? This raises a small interpretative problem. Did the apostle really mean "Paul" or

[18]Morris suggests: "If we are right in thinking of Chloe (I Cor. 1:11) as a Corinthian convert, she would have been a wealthy woman, owning slaves, and with interests in both Corinth and Ephesus (but she is perhaps more likely to have been an Ephesian with interests in Corinth). She is not likely to have been from the upper classes. The name 'Chloe' was an epithet of the goddess Demeter. Those who bore the names of deities were usually slaves or freed persons, consequently most commentators think of Chloe as a freedwoman, albeit a wealthy one." Morris, *Corinthians*, p. 19.

"Apollos" when he wrote those names, or did he use them symbolically? Later, he wrote, "And these things, brethren, I have in a figure transferred to myself and to Apollos for your sakes; that ye might learn in us not to think of men above that which is written" (4:6). Thus, it may mean that Paul wanted to solve the problem on the basis of principle, rather than personality; therefore, he chose not to mention the real names of the leaders of the Corinthian factions. In support for the literal meaning of the names, it is true that Paul, Apollos, and Peter had all visited Corinth (Acts 18:1, 24 — 19:1; I Cor. 9:5). Although they preached the same message, their rhetoric and personalities were different. The Corinthians may have rallied respectively behind those men whose ministries may have blessed them. What about the Christ-group? They may have completely rejected all human teachers and simply embraced the statements of Christ.[19] In either case, the problem was laid bare. Now, how would Paul solve it?

III. PROCEDURE IN CORRECTION (1:13–31)

Since disunity was the major sin at Corinth, Paul devoted more time and space to its solution than to any other problem. Actually, the first four chapters (1:13 — 4:21) are dedicated to the cure of the malady. In them, Paul tried to inform his readers about spiritual concepts. His theme was that repentance must be based on knowledge and that action must be guided by truth. He wanted to stimulate within them an awareness of: his involvement in their lives (1:13–17); the difference between human and divine wisdom (1:18–25); the nature of God's calling to salvation (1:26–31); the wisdom taught by the Holy Spirit (2:1–13); the three types of men in the world and in the church (2:14 8 3:4); the place of men in the ministry (3:5–9); their responsibility to build on their spiritual foundation (3:10–17); their utilization of all ministers (3:18 — 4:2); the judgment of their motivations by God (4:3–5); the real position of God's servants (4:6–13); and Paul's apostolic authority over them (4:14–21).

[19]One liberal view states this: "The words 'I belong to Christ' (1:12) are probably a gloss. Some pious scribe, noting the conflicting loyalties at Corinth, wrote the sentence in the margin of the manuscript as his own declaration of loyalty. A later copyist, thinking that it had been placed in the margin by Paul as a correction, incorporated it into the text." C. Milo Connick, *The New Testament*, p. 275.

A. Understand Paul's Involvement in Their Lives (1:13–17)

Immediately Paul disclaimed any blame for the split within the church. He neither created nor honored it; rather, he condemned it. He started off abruptly with a series of three questions.[20] They involve Christ in the essence of His person, the purpose of His redemptive death, and His exalted headship over His church. The three together have a familiar ring about them. After Peter had declared that Jesus was the Christ, the Son of God, Jesus predicted that He would build His church and that He would be crucified and resurrected to achieve that goal (Matt. 16:13–21).

1. Christ cannot be divided (1:13a)

"Divided? Does the Christ stand divided?" This is the force of the original Greek construction. The question could take either an affirmative or a negative answer, based upon the intent of the questioner.[21] From the actions of the Corinthians, an observer could conclude that Christ had been cut up into parts and distributed to the various factions. In fact, one of the groups had made an exclusive claim upon Him, saying, "I [am] of Christ" (1:12). Actually, their attitudes reflected a complete reversal of the facts. They failed to see that together they were the body of Christ, and individually members in particular (12:27).[22]

However, the question probably implies a negative answer. It is impossible for Christ to be divided. But to what does "Christ" refer? Does it refer to the eternal union of two natures, divine and human, within the single person of Christ? (Theologians call this concept the "hypostatic union." Christ is not two persons with a single nature nor a single person with a single, thean-

[20]Since there were no marks of punctuation in the original writings, some have seen them as three exclamations: "Christ is divided! Paul was crucified for you! You were baptized in Paul's name!" Others view them as a combination of interrogation and exclamation: "Is Christ divided?!"

[21]Questions that have *ou* imply a positive answer, whereas questions that have *mē* imply a negative one. However, neither *ou* nor *mē* occurs with this first question.

[22]The word for "in particular" (*merous*) is based upon the verb "divided" (*memeristai*).

Paul's Third Missionary Journey

thropic nature. At the incarnation, God the Son, a person with a divine nature, took to Himself a perfect human nature. This union was not erased at His death or resurrection, nor will it ever be.) Or, does the question refer to the mystical body of Christ, the true church, into which the Corinthian believers had been baptized in the Holy Spirit (12:13)? Paul wrote elsewhere, "There is one body . . ." (Eph. 4:4). This spiritual unity cannot be dissolved by practical differences; however, Christians must do their utmost "to keep the unity of the Spirit in the bond of peace" (Eph. 4:3). Both of these concepts are Biblically correct.

2. Faith in Paul cannot save (1:13b)

"Was Paul crucified for you?" The question expects a negative answer. Paul was himself a sinner, the chief of sinners by his own confession (I Tim. 1:15). How could he die vicariously? How could he bear the sin, guilt, and penalty of other men when he could not even redeem himself (cf. Phil. 3:7–9)? If men exalted Paul for their salvation experience through his evangelistic preaching, they were wrong. This was the point Paul wanted to communicate. Trust in man will not save anyone; therefore, do not exalt a human leader, no matter how much of a blessing he has been to you.

3. Men cannot be baptized in the name of Paul (1:13b–16)

The resurrected Christ gave this commission to the apostles: "Go ye therefore, and teach [disciple] all nations, baptizing them in the name of the Father, and of the Son, and of the Holy Ghost: Teaching them to observe all things whatsoever I have commanded you . . ." (Matt. 28:19–20a). Baptism was essential for total obedience or discipleship, but not as a means of salvation. Consequently, all converts were immediately baptized to manifest publicly their faith in the crucified, resurrected Christ (Acts 2:41; 8:12, 35–39; 9:18; 10:48). In his missionary travels, Paul followed this same procedure (Acts 16:15, 33; 19:5). His question, therefore, expressed surprise and shock: ". . . or were ye baptized in the name of Paul?" The question naturally implies a negative answer.

When Paul evangelized Corinth during his second journey, many believed and were baptized (Acts 18:8); however, the apostle had personally baptized very few. His associates, Silas and Timothy, were probably given this responsibility. This practice was not rare; Jesus Christ did not baptize anyone either (John 4:1–2). Paul's action demonstrated that although the ordinance was important, the person who administered it was not. In retrospect, Paul was thankful for the providential direction of his practice. He did not want believers to align themselves behind him simply because he had baptized them.

Perhaps this is how the factions started. Those who were baptized by Apollos (or by one who had been baptized by Apollos) contended with those who had been baptized directly by Paul (or by one who had been baptized by Paul). The same would be true of the Peter group. Paul had personally baptized Crispus, Gaius, and the household of Stephanas. Crispus had been the chief ruler of the Corinthian synagogue before his conversion (Acts 18:8). During his third journey, Paul stayed in the house of Gaius when he visited Corinth, a house that also served as the meeting place for the church (Rom. 16:33).

Stephanas[23] was one of the three church messengers who had brought a gift of money and the letter of inquiry to Paul (16:17). His family was identified as "the firstfruits of Achaia" (16:15); thus, they were among Paul's first converts, if not the first. On the basis of direct baptism, the Pauline faction would have to be very small.

Paul could not remember the names of others whom he had baptized and/or could not remember whether he had baptized any more (in numbers). Thus, he did not count numbers or keep track of names, even though some in the church were bragging about their relationship to him. His lack of remembrance[24] thus formed a mild rebuke of their pride; ironically, he could not name his followers.

Paul was not after personal prestige. He pointed men to Christ, not to himself. He baptized in Christ's name, not in his own. According to the papyri, the name of a king or a god stood for the power and authority of that king or god.[25]

4. Paul came to evangelize (1:17)

Paul claimed that Christ did not send him to be a baptizer, but to be a preacher. Robertson correctly observed, "Paul casts no reflection on baptism, for he could not with his conception of it as the picture of the new life in Christ (Rom. 6:2–6), but he clearly denies here that he considers baptism essential to the remission of sin or the means of obtaining forgiveness."[26] Thus the gospel, which "is the power of God unto salvation to everyone that believeth" (Rom. 1:16), does not incorporate baptism as a necessary step. At the same time, Paul did not declare

---

[23]Since Stephanas was not listed with Crispus and Gaius, some have speculated that his name was mentioned as an afterthought, perhaps at the prodding of Stephanas himself.

[24]Inspiration thus involves the inclusion of one's own forgetfulness. Hodge wrote: "From these sources we learn that it [inspiration] was an influence which rendered its recipients infallible, but it did not render them omniscient. They were preserved from asserting error, but they were not enabled either to know or to remember all things." Hodge, *Corinthians*, p. 16.

[25]A. T. Robertson, *Word Pictures in the New Testament*, 4:75.

[26]Ibid., p. 76.

that baptism was not for this age.[27] Furthermore, Paul *did* baptize (1:14, 16), and so did his associates.

Again, he asserted that he had been directly sent by Christ. The verb for "sent" (*apesteilen*) is the root for the noun "apostle." The invested authority of Christ in Paul can be seen throughout his writings.

Paul also knew that he was responsible to Christ not only for *what* he preached, but for *how* he preached. Content and method must harmonize. Faulty content is heretical (e.g., denial of Christ's deity or His bodily resurrection), and so is wrong methodology. Evangelicals too often condemn the former and approve the latter. If worldly logic or non-Scriptural reasons are used to move sinners to a decision for Christ, then the cross has been stripped of its divine significance. Morris commented: "The faithful preaching of the cross results in men ceasing to put their trust in any human device, and relying rather on God's work in Christ. A reliance on rhetoric would cause men to trust in men, the very antithesis of what the preaching of the cross is meant to effect."[28]

Thus, Paul wanted the Corinthians to see that the person of Christ had sent him to focus men's hearts on the cross of Christ. In the church, there should be loyalty only to Him, not to His human instruments.

B. Understand the Difference Between Human and Divine Wisdom (1:18–25)

Verse 17 serves as a fitting introduction to this section of Paul's argument. In it, he referred to "wisdom of words" (*sophia logou*) which is contrasted now with the "preaching of the cross." Literally, Paul wrote "the word of the cross" (*ho logos tou staurou*). What is the difference, then, between those two "words"? It is as vast as the gulf between heaven and hell.

1. Human wisdom is foolish (1:18–20)

There are only two groups of people in the world: those

---

[27]If that had been so, he would have used the aorist infinitive (*baptisai*) rather than the present infinitive (*baptizein*).

[28]Morris, *Corinthians,* p. 42.

"that perish" and those "which are saved." Men and women are *now* in either a lost or saved standing before God.[29] Their spiritual position determines their evaluation of the cross. The perishing group views the fact and significance of Christ's death as silly or absurd. The English word "moron" is based upon the Greek word for "foolishness" (*mōria*). Note the order here. The unsaved are not perishing because they regard the cross to be foolishness; rather, they treat it with mental disgust because they are already perishing. Boyer wrote, "The word 'perish' does not indicate extinction, but ruin; not loss of *being*, but loss of *well-being*."[30] It is translated elsewhere as "lost" (Luke 19:10; II Cor. 4:3). On the other hand, the saved group sees the cross as "the power of God unto salvation to everyone that believeth" (cf. Rom. 1:16). The word of the cross is neither good advice to men nor a message about God's power; it *is* God's power. Boyer correctly observed, "The vindication of the cross is not wisdom, that it *makes sense*; but power, it *works*."[31] It changes lives. It makes saints out of sinners (cf. 6:9–11), preachers out of blasphemers (I Tim. 1:12–13).

For support of the preceding thesis, Paul referred to an event from Israel's past (1:19; cf. Isa. 29:14). When the Assyrians threatened Judah, the counselors of the Jewish king advised an alliance with Egypt. This proposal was opposed by the prophet Isaiah who appealed to Judah to trust in God alone. Isaiah's counsel was mocked by the scribes of Jerusalem. Egypt never came to Judah's rescue, but God did in a miraculous fashion. In one night, His angel killed 186,000 Assyrians; in the morning, the pagan army retreated (Isa. 37:36–37). The principle that lay beneath that historical event is also true of attitudes toward God and the cross today. Men have devised their own programs of personal and social redemption in which they trust themselves and not God. Such plans only lead to death (Prov. 14:12).

[29]The verbs "perish" and "saved" are both present participles. Paul did not describe a future possibility, but rather a present reality.

[30]James L. Boyer, *For a World Like Ours*, p. 34.

[31]Ibid., p. 35.

Various scenes of an Assyrian army. This relief was recovered from Ashurbanipal's palace at Nineveh.

The Old Testament quotation then led to a series of four rhetorical questions (1:20; cf. Isa. 19:12; 33:18). The "wise" refers to Gentile philosophers, like those who mocked Paul for preaching the resurrection of Christ (Acts 17:22–32). The scribe originally was the Jewish secretary who prepared and issued decrees in the name of the king (II Sam. 8:17; 20:25; II Kings 12:10; 19:2). Later, they were known as learned in the law because they transcribed, expounded, and administered it. The "disputer of this age" involves both Jews and Gentiles (Acts 6:9; 9:29; 17:18; 28:29). One age passes into the next with the former age forgotten; the same is true of its disputers (Eccles. 1:4–11). Where are they? When God's wisdom and power are manifested, foolish men disappear. The fourth question summarizes this section. Men regard the cross, the greatest display of God's power and wisdom, as foolish; but the opposite is true. In the cross, "God made foolish the wisdom" of men. The wisest of men, unaided by the Spirit of God, become spiritual dunces when they try to understand *why* Christ died.

2. Human wisdom cannot save (1:21–23)

19

The preceding section ended with a question; this section begins with the answer, introduced by the explanatory connective "for." In His sovereign wisdom, God planned that exalted human wisdom would never be the instrument for knowing God and being saved (1:21). Even though God's wisdom and power are displayed in creation, men have misunderstood, ignored, perverted, and rejected those truths (Rom. 1:18–32). Only a divinely enlightened person can perceive God's glory in His handiwork (Ps. 19:1). In His free, sovereign choice, God was also pleased to save men by that *message* which men thought to be foolish: *the cross.* The word "preaching" (*kērygmatos*) does not refer to a special technique of oral communication; rather, it pertains to the content of what is declared. God also planned to save men by that *method* which men thought to be simple: *faith.* Men are not saved by what they know, but by whom they believe.

Paul argued that finite, sinful men cannot dictate to an infinite, holy God what they want from God before they will believe (1:22). The Jews had always requested a sign (empirical evidence) before they would believe. Moses had to perform signs before the enslaved Jews would accept his divinely appointed leadership (Exod. 4:29–31). During Christ's earthly ministry, Israel did not discern the signs of the times (Matt. 16:3). When they deviously asked for another sign, Christ pointed out that the next sign for Israel would be that of Jonah and the fish, an event which typified His coming death and resurrection (Matt. 12:38–40; 16:4). In their willful rebellion, they even attempted to explain the empty tomb by the theft of the body by the disciples (Matt. 28:11–15).

On the other hand, the Gentiles wanted rational proof ("wisdom") before they would accept. The Greek philosophers mocked Paul when he preached the resurrection (Acts 17:32). After hearing Paul's defense of the faith, the Roman governor Festus declared, "Paul, thou art beside thyself; much learning doth make thee mad" (Acts 26:24). The Jews said, "Show me." The Gentiles reacted, "Let me investigate."

In response, Paul did not honor their requests (1:23). The connective "but" shows the contrast. He *preached*; he did not perform sign miracles for the Jews in the synagogue, nor did he discuss rational proofs with the Greeks. His message contained what men needed, not what they wanted. He preached "Christ crucified."[32] The double reaction to the message was similar, yet different. The Jews regarded it as a "stumbling block" (literally, a "scandal," *skandalon*) because they thought that the Messiah would bring political victory and live forever (Matt. 27:42; John 12:34). The same word is used for "trap" or "snare" in the papyri. The Gentiles regarded the message as foolishness. They viewed a crucified criminal — which Christ was under Roman law — as morally offensive and as an evidence of physical weakness. How could the blood of such a person remove sin, give righteousness, and guarantee hope beyond the grave? To them, it was absurd.

3. Divine wisdom can save (1:24–25)

The preceding two sections viewed the divine program of salvation from the perspective of unsaved men; now Paul looked at it through the understanding of those who were called to salvation (cf. 1:2, 18). The saved Jew, who wanted a sign before, can now see the real power of God displayed in Christ's triumph over sin and death in His death and resurrection. The saved Gentile, who once sought rational arguments, now marvels at God's sophisticated solution for the problem of evil (cf. Rom. 11:33).

Paul's conclusion to this paragraph contains a striking paradox. What unsaved men viewed as foolish is really wise, and what they deprecated as weak is actually strong. The two phrases "foolishness of God" and "weakness of God" do not refer to God's attributes of omnipotence and omniscience; rather, they are synonyms for the death of Christ.

C. Understand the Nature of God's Calling (1:26–31)

Robertson described this paragraph as "a clinching illustration of Paul's argument, an *argumentum ad hominem*."[33] The connective "for" joins the two sections, especially since the subject of the Corinthians' calling was reintroduced (1:26; cf. 1:2, 24). The

---

[32]The verbal adjective "crucified" is a perfect passive participle (*estaurōmenon*). Thus, Christ's death was permanent in its efficacy and effects.

[33]Robertson, *Word Pictures*, p. 80.

calling does not refer to a person's vocation or life-style; rather it denotes the call of God by the Holy Spirit through the Scriptures. In their carnality, the Corinthians had forgotten what they once were before God saved them. They needed to be reminded of this.

1. It is not based on man's position (1:26)

God is no respecter of persons (cf. James 2:1–9). He does not favor the rich over the poor, nor does He favor the poor over the rich. Man's status in this life neither attracts nor repels God. His choice to salvation is entirely apart from these considerations.

In the Corinthian membership, there were not many wise, mighty, or noble persons, as the world uses those terms (the phrase "after the flesh" goes with all three groups). The "wise" refers to the *intellect* of men — what they have learned. The "mighty" points to the *influence* of men — that which they have gained through political or military conquests. The "noble" denotes the *inheritance* of men — the status of birth into well-known families. Note that Paul used "many" rather than "any." Some wise, mighty, and noble people *are* called to salvation by God. The Corinthian church possessed some who might be thus described, including: Crispus, the chief ruler of the synagogue (Acts 18:8); Gaius, Paul's host (Rom. 16:23); Erastus, the chamberlain of Corinth (Rom. 16:23); and possibly the wealthy Chloe (1:11).

2. It manifests divine interest (1:27)

The verb "hath chosen" occurs twice in this verse and once in the next. It translates the Greek word *exelexato,* which implies that God has chosen men *in His own interest.* Salvation, therefore, is not man-centered, but God-centered. Elsewhere Paul wrote: "Blessed be the God and Father of our Lord Jesus Christ, who hath blessed us with all spiritual blessings in heavenly places in Christ: According as he hath chosen [same verb] us in him before the foundation of the world, that we should be holy and without blame before him in love" (Eph. 1:3–4). God chose to save, love, and bless as a demonstration of His gracious will — *not* because we deserved to be chosen. There was nothing in the nature or actions of men that merited God's favor.

3. It is contrary to the expectations of men (1:27–28)

God's choices are just the opposite of what men would do if they were given the divine prerogative to choose. They are also just the opposite of what men would expect God to do. This is why God "confounds" and "brings to nought" the logic of men through His redemptive program of the cross and through those who accept His grace by faith. Hodge claimed that God wanted to convince the world "of the little value of the things on which they prided themselves, and by exalting over them those whom they despised."[34]

The contrasts are apparent. The wise are confounded by the choice of the unlearned (the foolish). The strong (mighty)[35] marvel at the choice of the physically disabled (the weak). The well-born aristocrats are baffled by the selection of the base low-born (literally "no birth," agenē). There is a declining order of importance from "base" to "despised" to "things which are nought." This includes slaves, the poor, barbarians, and other looked-down-upon groups.

4. It removes the basis for human boasting (1:29)

God chose "that no flesh should glory in his presence." How clear and firm that statement is! In describing God's plan of salvation, three times Paul inserted "to the praise of his glory" (Eph. 1:6, 12, 14). No man, regardless of achievements either before or after salvation, should dare to brag about himself in the presence of God on earth or in heaven. In later correspondence, Paul wrote, "But we have this treasure in earthen vessels, that the excellency of the power may be of God, and not of us" (II Cor. 4:7). The Corinthians and all saved people need to realize that they are what they are by the grace of God (cf. 15:10).

[34]Hodge, Corinthians, p. 25.

[35]The word for "mighty" (ischyra) in verse 27 is different from the word for "mighty" (dynatoi) in verse 26.

5. It will result in the glorification of God (1:30–31)

The connective "but" shows the contrast between those who glory in the flesh and those who glory in God. Christians should glorify God because the source of their spiritual blessings is the Father ("of Him") and the sphere of those blessings is the Son ("in Christ Jesus"). Thus, it is because of their position in Christ that God can impute to them wisdom concerning His ways ("made unto us"). The four words describing the believer's possessions are not equal or coordinate. Rather, the imputed wisdom is defined by the other three words. Those who are called recognize wisdom in the crucified Christ (1:24) because they have received total salvation: "righteousness," which guarantees an acceptable position before God and deliverance from the penalty of sin; "sanctification," which provides victory over the practice of sin; and "redemption," which assures the believer of release from the presence of sinful effects in his body. God's wisdom thus deals with the past, present, and future of each Christian. In response to such gracious imputation, men are to "glory in the Lord." The Old Testament quotation (Jer. 9:24) referred to glorying in Jehovah; thus Paul equated Jehovah with the Lord Jesus Christ, a proof of His deity (cf. 1:2, 3, 8, 9, 10).

QUESTIONS FOR DISCUSSION

1. Are the gospel songs which exalt only the name "Jesus" consistent with Paul's designation of Him as "Lord Jesus Christ"?

2. What is the difference between Biblical sainthood and Roman Catholic Sainthood?

3. Are church splits ever justified? Do you believe that the existence of denominations is pleasing to God?

4. Should anonymous reports about sinning Christians ever be accepted as true? What should be done with a person who bears false witness?

5. Do evangelicals sometimes use worldly methods and logic in presenting the gospel? If so, what are they? How can this be avoided?

6. In what ways do modern people treat the cross as foolishness?

7. Should churches move to the suburbs when neighborhoods change? What contemporary groups correspond to what Paul terms the "wise," "mighty," "noble," "base," and "despised"?

2

The Relationship of
Wisdom to Spirituality
I Corinthians 2:1 — 3:4

In his attempt to correct the carnal divisiveness of the Corinthians, Paul had already informed them of his involvement in their lives (1:13–17), the difference between human and divine wisdom (1:18–25), and the nature of God's calling to salvation (1:26–31). In this new section, he advanced his solution by two more steps.[1] First, he pointed out their need of divine wisdom which is communicated to men only by the Spirit of God (2:1–13), and second, he showed that there were three types of men within the world and possibly within their church (2:14 — 3:4).

I. NATURE OF DIVINE WISDOM (2:1–13)

Paul was acutely aware of the distinction between human logic and divine wisdom. Unaided human wisdom ridicules the message of Christ's death and resurrection (1:18), but the regenerated mind perceives the divine logic behind that proclamation. Paul wanted his readers to repudiate that wisdom which they exalted in their unsaved condition and to manifest divine wisdom. Thus, in the first part of this chapter, he described the nature of divine wisdom in three basic areas.

A. Divine Wisdom Was Used in Paul's Evangelism (2:1–5)

The temporal clause ("when I came to you") refers to Paul's

---

[1]The continuity between the two chapters can be seen in the use of the mild connective "and." Also, the familiar address "brethren" was used several times in the first chapter (1:10, 11, 26).

second missionary journey when he alone[2] entered into the city of Corinth and began a ministry which lasted at least eighteen months (Acts 18:1–18). During that time, he preached in the synagogue to Jews and to Greek proselytes (Acts 18:4), in the private home of Justus to pagan Corinthians (Acts 18:7–8), and doubtless in other places to the entire strata of Corinthian society.

1. His method (2:1)

Paul claimed that he did not use human rhetoric ("excellency of speech") and human wisdom in his preaching. In what he said ("wisdom") and how he said it ("speech"), he did not employ what man had developed or desired. Some commentators have suggested that Paul *did* use human logic and wisdom in his unsuccessful attempt to reach the Athenian philosophers (Acts 17:22–34), that he learned his lesson not to rely upon human methods, and that he therefore switched his tactics when he came to Corinth.[3] However, Paul clearly pointed out that the finest mind and the most eloquent speech that men could develop, in themselves, are inadequate in the proclamation of spiritual truth.[4]

The content of Paul's declaration was the "testimony of God."[5] It could refer to what God Himself had spoken or to Paul's witness concerning God. Both, of course, are true. We must preach only that which God has spoken (cf. Acts 1:8).

2. His message (2:2)

The connective "for" introduces the reason behind his

[2]Note the constant references to "I" and "my" in these verses.

[3]Harry Ironside, *I Corinthians*, p. 79.

[4]Connick sees this phrase as "an indirect put-down, perhaps, of the lustrous language of Apollos." C. Milo Connick, *The New Testament*, p. 275. However, this is pure speculation. Paul and Apollos complemented each other's ministry (3:5–6, 22; 16:12).

[5]There is a slight textual problem here. Some Greek manuscripts read "mystery" rather than "testimony." The mystery of God doubtless refers to Christ (Col. 1:27; 2:2–3). The testimony of God would refer to what God has done in Christ. Basically, there is no great difference between the two phrases.

method. Before he had preached his first message in Corinth, Paul had determined that his content would be a simple, clear, and frank presentation of both the person of Christ, including His deity, humanity, and messiahship ("save Jesus Christ"), and His redemptive work, involving the death and resurrection ("and Him crucified"). To do this, Paul "reasoned" (*dielegeto*, Acts 18:4),[6] "persuaded" (*epeithen*, Acts 18:4), and "testified" (*diamartyromenos*, Acts 18:5). This was no mere statement of facts; his message conveyed spiritual, Biblical, and logical arguments. Logic, divine not human, can and must saturate our sermons and witness.

Grosheide claims that the prepositional phrase "among you" cannot mean that Paul chose a special manner of preaching for the Corinthians, but it indicates that what he did at Corinth he did everywhere else and the Corinthians should know that."[7] Paul was consistent. His message remained the same even though he adapted his methods of presentation to his audiences.

3. His manner (2:3)

Three prepositional phrases ("in weakness," "in fear," and "in much trembling") indicate the threefold manner in which Paul appeared at Corinth. They can be interpreted in two different ways.

First, Paul's use of these phrases may point out his acknowledgement of his human insufficiency for such a task. He was physically weak, having traveled for some time and distance (Acts 15:40 — 18:1) and having been beaten and jailed at Philippi (Acts 16:22–24). The words "in fear and in much trembling" thus may have manifested his acute awareness of his relationship to God and of his awesome responsibility to preach. These words do not always mean an emotional frailty or fear of men and circumstances. Believers are commanded to work out their own salvation "with fear and trembling" (Phil. 2:12). In the same attitude, servants are to obey their masters as they would Christ (Eph. 6:5). These phrases, therefore, can contain positive,

---

[6]The English words "dialogue" and "dialectic" are based on this Greek word. It connotes a thorough, logical presentation.

[7]F. W. Grosheide, *Commentary on the First Epistle to the Corinthians*, p. 59.

commendable qualities. The next two verses (2:4–5) would support this thesis.

A second view sees these three phrases as Paul's admission of inner fears. Various reasons have been suggested for his fears. He was beaten in Philippi, driven out of both Thessalonica and Berea, mocked in Athens, and had arrived alone in Corinth. Some have speculated that his weakness was caused by his unimpressive physical appearance and speech (II Cor. 10:10), by anxiety over what was happening to Timothy and Silas in Macedonia, by the wickedness of Corinth, and by a persistent physical infirmity (Gal. 4:13). Concerning the discharge of his ministry, Paul did admit, "We are troubled on every side, yet not distressed; we are perplexed, but not in despair; persecuted, but not forsaken; cast down, but not destroyed" (II Cor. 4:8–9). In the midst of his ministry at Corinth, Paul *did* need divine encouragement. Luke wrote:

> Then spake the Lord to Paul in the night by a vision, Be not afraid, but speak, and hold not thy peace:
>
> For I am with thee, and no man shall set on thee to hurt thee; for I have much people in this city. Acts 18:9–10

These verses reveal a concern for personal, physical safety, a fear of men, and a reluctance to preach. Later, Paul received similar comfort (Acts 23:11; 27:24). In anticipation of a future visit to Corinth, Paul confessed to inner fears that were relieved by God (II Cor. 7:5–7). It is true that the Holy Spirit directed men, when writing the Scriptures, to write about their faults as well as their virtues.

4. His means (2:4)

Paul again affirmed that his speech (how he spoke)[8] and his preaching (what he said)[9] did not reflect human means, but rather divine enablement. The Gnostics beguiled men with "enticing words" (Col. 2:4), but Paul did not. The adjective "enticing" (*peithois*) conveys the idea of persuasive speech used by de-

[8]The word "speech" is logos, based on the verb *legō*, meaning "I say."

[9]The word "preaching" seems to refer to oral techniques, but the Greek word *kērugma* emphasizes the content rather than the style of what is being said.

baters or salesmen. Although the apostle "persuaded" (*peithō*, Acts 18:4) the Jews and the Greeks of Corinth, he did not use rational and emotional appeals that were devoid of Biblical content or spiritual thrust.

The strong adversative "but" (*alla*) shows the contrast between the negative and the positive means of his preaching. It reveals a difference between persuasion and demonstration. The word for "demonstration" (*apodeixei*) was used legally for proofs produced in a court of law. Paul's proofs of the authenticity of his message could be seen in the changed lives of his converts who had been delivered from sin and idolatry and who had spiritual direction and goals. The Holy Spirit and power cannot be separated (Acts 1:8). Since Paul was controlled by the Spirit, he was enabled to say what had to be said, to present it in the right way, and to reap the results of spiritual transformation. This was the secret of his success. To the Thessalonians he wrote, "For our gospel came not unto you in word only, but also in power, and in the Holy Ghost . . ." (I Thess. 1:5). He later explained what he meant in that verse: " . . . when ye received the word of God which ye heard of us, ye received it not as the word of men, but as it is in truth, the word of God, which effectually worketh also in you that believe" (I Thess. 2:13). This demonstration was not only inward and subjective in the regenerated lives of the believers, but also outward and objective in the supernatural authentication of Paul's apostolic message through miracles and the impartation of spiritual gifts.

5. His motive (2:5)

The purpose for using divine wisdom rather than human logic is introduced by the word "that" (*hina*). Paul wanted their saving faith in Jesus Christ, the persuasion of the heart and the mind which leads to a commitment of the will, to be a result of divine persuasion ("power of God"), not human ("wisdom of men"). Paul was not after superficial decisions; rather, he desired genuine, God-produced experiences in the lives of his listeners.

B. Divine Wisdom Is Unique (2:6–9)

Paul was not against wisdom *per se;* he used it. Rather, he

Alabaster vases from Corinth, ca. 600 B.C.

Corinthian oenochoes.

31

opposed "the wisdom of this world" — namely, human wisdom. To him, there was a great difference between the two. To point out his exaltation of genuine wisdom, he began this section with this literal translation, "But wisdom we do speak." The direct object ("wisdom") of the verb is placed first in the sentence, thus receiving great emphasis. Paul, then, made nine consecutive observations about this wisdom.

1. Divine wisdom can only be known by the perfect (2:6a)

This descriptive phrase, "them that are perfect" (*tois teleiois*), refers to believers who have matured in the Christian faith and who are still growing. It excludes the unsaved, the carnal babes in Christ (3:1), and those complacent Christians who feel that they have arrived. Paul exhorted the Corinthians to be men (*teleioi*) in their understanding (14:20). The eventual goal for each believer is total spiritual manhood or full conformity to the image of Christ (Eph. 4:13). Paul was mature, and yet he knew that he was not yet perfect in the ultimate sense (Phil. 3:12). A perfect Christian is a mature believer who has experienced spiritual growth, who has applied the Word of God to moral decisions, and who has the ability to teach others what God has taught him (Heb. 5:11–14 — translated as "full age"). The switch from the singular ("I") to the plural ("we") indicates that Paul regarded his associates and himself as among the perfect in this sense.

2. Divine wisdom is not of this age nor of the princes of this age (2:6b)

The word for "world" is *aiōn*, not *kosmos*. It is a time word, better translated as "age." The "wisdom of this age" reflects thinking within boundaries. Recall the great thinkers of past ages whose ideas of science, medicine, and philosophy have been disproved by the discoveries of subsequent ages. Genuine wisdom transcends the ages of time and is eternal. The "princes of this age" could refer to either demonic rulers (Eph. 6:12; Col. 2:15) or to national political leaders (Acts 3:17). In this case it probably refers to the latter (cf. 2:8). Unsaved kings are totally unaware of the purpose of history and of God's redemptive program for nations and individuals. They see no relationship between the civil and the spiritual. The temporal character of political wisdom can be seen in the fact that rulers and systems of government are constantly changing and disappearing.[10] Biblical prophecy (Dan. 2; 7) has foreseen the rise and fall of nations, climaxing in the clash between Jesus Christ and the wicked powers at Armageddon.

3. Divine wisdom is God's wisdom (2:7a)

The strong adversative "but" contrasts the temporal wisdom of this age with the timeless wisdom of the eternal God. Also, the possessive "of God" is emphasized in the Greek word order. Paul and his associates spoke God's wisdom, not their own.

4. Divine wisdom is in a mystery (2:7a)

The word translated "mystery" (*mystērion*)[11] is based on an ancient word which conveyed the idea of shutting the mouth. The Biblical use is that that which was once silent is now vocal. Scriptural mysteries are divine truths once unknown and unspoken by men in past ages, but now proclaimed and understood by yielded believers.

5. Divine wisdom is hidden (2:7a)[12]

The redemptive truth of the gospel remains hidden to the lost of the world whose minds have been blinded by Satan (II Cor. 4:3–4). The truth of New Testament Christianity was also hidden from past generations of believers, but it is now revealed (Eph. 3:5, 9; Col. 1:26). Paul praised God for this disclosure (Rom. 16:25–27).

6. Divine wisdom manifests the eternal plan of God (2:7b)

Concerning believers, God "did predestinate [them] to be conformed to the image of his Son" (Rom. 8:29). This predestination of believers was included within God's foreordained wis-

[10]The phrase "that come to nought" (*tōn katargoumenōn*) is a genitive, plural participle agreeing with "rulers," not with "world."

[11]It is used twenty-seven times in the New Testament: three times in the Gospels; twenty times in Paul's letters; and four times in the Revelation.

[12]The perfect passive participle *tēn apokekrymmenēn* refers to the feminine noun "wisdom," not to the neuter word "mystery."

dom which was decreed before the ages of time began.[13] The incarnation, death, and resurrection of Jesus Christ were also foreknown and foreordained (Acts 2:23; I Peter 1:20). The purpose of this determined, wise plan was "unto our glory." God has already positionally glorified each believer (Rom. 8:30), but practically, he must wait to share in the glory of an immortal, incorruptible body (Rom. 8:18).

7. Divine wisdom was unknown to the rulers who crucified Christ (2:8)

Paul made this assertion, then proved it with a hypothetical argument.[14] When first placed on the cross, Jesus prayed, "Father, forgive them; for they know not what they do" (Luke 23:34).[15] Not one of the officials responsible for the illegal trials of Christ (Annas, Caiaphas, Pilate, Herod Antipas) perceived the real identity of Christ, nor did they understand the significance of His presence in their midst. Some of His followers, including the apostles and Mary, did; but this wisdom was hidden to the lost rulers. In his second sermon, Peter explained to the Jews, "And now, brethren, I wot [know] that through ignorance ye did it, as did also your rulers" (Acts 3:17). Paul then cited the crucifixion as proof of the rulers' ignorance. What is so amazing is the fact that God worked out His wise plan in and through human ignorance. Wicked hands of blinded men crucified Christ, but this is exactly what God had willed (Acts 2:22–23). Nevertheless, God holds men spiritually responsible for their sinful deeds.

The title for Christ, "the Lord of glory," is a proof of His deity. God is depicted as "the God of glory" (Acts 7:2) and "the Father of Glory" (Eph. 1:17). The "King of glory" (Ps. 24) is

[13]The phrase "before the world" is based on the Greek *pro tōn aiōnōn*, better translated as "before the ages."

[14]The connective "for" introduces a conditional clause which is contrary to fact. Such clauses begin with "if" (*ei*) and use secondary tenses in both the protasis ("for had they known it") and the apodosis ("they would not have crucified the Lord of glory").

[15]The two words for "know" are different: *oida* in Luke 23:34 and *ginōskō* in I Corinthians 2:8.

none other than Christ. The fact that He was crucified demonstrates His human nature. Thus, the perception of divine wisdom involves the recognition of the hypostatic union, the union of two natures (divine and human) within the single person of Christ.

8. Divine wisdom is contrary to man's experience (2:9a)

Sense perception is seen in the references to the eye and to the ear, whereas rationalizations stem from the heart. Leon Morris observed, "*Heart* stood rather for the whole of a man's inner life, including thought and will as well as the emotions."[16] To prove his point, Paul pointed to the Old Testament (Isa. 52:15; 64:4; 65:17).[17] Grammatically, there is a slight problem with the quotation. Do the relative clauses (introduced by "the things which") go with "we speak" (2:7) or "God hath revealed" (2:10)? Thus, we speak what eye has not seen nor ear heard, *or* God has revealed what eye has not seen nor ear heard. Both, of course, were true in the apostle's experience. He could only speak what God had already revealed.

9. Divine wisdom is prepared by God "only for them that love Him" (2:9b)

To the Romans, Paul affirmed, "And we know that all things work together for good to them that love God, to them who are the called according to his purpose" (Rom. 8:28). Thus, the prepared things are God's redemptive plans for each individual, including foreknowledge, predestination, sonship, calling, justification, and glorification (Rom. 8:29–30).

C. Divine Wisdom Is Centered in the Holy Spirit (2:10–13)

Just as power or enablement cannot be separated from the Holy Spirit (2:4; cf. Acts 1:8), so genuine wisdom cannot be divorced from Him. You cannot have one without the other. Paul had just introduced the person of the Spirit into the context

[16]Leon Morris, *The First Epistle of Paul to the Corinthians,* p. 57.

[17]Robertson wrote: "It is not certain where Paul derives this quotation as Scripture. . . . It is likely that Paul here combines freely Isa. 64:4; 65:17; and 52:15 in a sort of catena or free chain of quotations as he does in Rom. 3:10-18." A. T. Robertson, *Word Pictures in the New Testament,* 4:85.

of divine wisdom (2:4). Now he wanted to show how essential the ministry of the Spirit was in obtaining spiritual wisdom. He emphasized three areas.

1. The Holy Spirit is essential in revelation (2:10–11)

Divine wisdom has been revealed by God to believers through the Holy Spirit. The words "unto us" stand first in the Greek sentence; thus, the emphasis rests upon the recipients of the revelation. That which remains hidden and unknown to the world God has revealed, but only to the saved.

All three persons within the trinitarian oneness are involved in divine revelation. In this verse, the "Spirit" is the personal agent through whom the Father has revealed truth. Jesus prayed, "I thank thee, O Father, Lord of heaven and earth, because thou hast hid these things from the wise and prudent, and hast revealed them unto babes" (Matt. 11:25). Later He added, ". . . neither knoweth any man the Father, save the Son, and he to whomsoever the Son will reveal him" (Matt. 11:27). The identity of Jesus Christ cannot be known apart from the revelation of the Father (Matt. 16:17). The Book of Hebrews begins, "God, who at sundry times and in divers manners spake in time past unto the fathers by the prophets, hath in these last days spoken unto us by his Son" (Heb. 1:1–2a). Revelation, thus, is the communication of divine truth from God to man. It has taken several forms: creation, direct oral pronouncements, visions, dreams, the incarnation, and the Scriptures. Paul claimed that the Bible was God-breathed,[18] or "given by inspiration of God" (II Tim. 3:16). Peter elaborated, "For the prophecy came not in old time by the will of man: but holy men of God spake as they were moved by the Holy Ghost" (II Peter 1:21). The Bible, then, not only contains revelation; it *is* divine revelation.

The reason why the Spirit has been involved in revelation is introduced by the explanatory word "for" (2:10b, 11a). It is simple; the Spirit knows everything about God because He Himself is God. Morris commented: "*Searcheth* does not mean that the Spirit searches with a view to obtaining information, Rather it is

---

[18]The phrase "is given by inspiration of God" is the translation of one Greek word *theopneustos*. Literally, it means "God-breathed." The written Word is just as much the Word of God as the direct spoken Word of God.

a way of saying that He penetrates into *all things*."[19] The Spirit knows God, God knows the Spirit, and the Spirit knows us (Rom. 8:26–27). The "deep things of God" specifically refers to those matters that pertain to God's redemptive program of the ages (cf. "all things" in Rom. 8:28). In concluding his exposition of salvation, Paul marveled: "O the depth of the riches both of the wisdom and knowledge of God! how unsearchable are his judgments, and his ways past finding out!" (Rom. 11:33).

For further proof of the Spirit's omniscience, Paul drew an analogy from the relationship of the human spirit to man's total being (2:11). Ironside commented: "The spirit is the personality. It is that which differentiates him from the lower creation, enables him to think, to weigh evidence, to reason, to investigate."[20] Both God and man are personal beings; thus, both have the innate ability to know themselves and to disclose themselves to others. They are not known as objects are known, from outside observation (I Sam. 16:7; cf. I Sam. 1:10–16). By the very constitution of man, self-consciousness resides within the man. Solomon observed, "The spirit of man is the candle of the Lord, searching all the inward parts of the belly" (Prov. 20:27). However, there is a basic difference between the relationship of the human spirit to man and that of the Holy Spirit to God. Note the words "which is in him" for the human spirit. A comparable phrase is not attached to the Spirit of God. Thus, the Spirit of God should not be equated with God's own self-consciousness.[21] Just as the human spirit knows and reveals itself, so the divine Spirit knows and reveals the things of God.

2. The Holy Spirit is essential in illumination (2:12)

How can men know what the Spirit knows and what God has revealed through the Spirit? They must have their spiritual understanding illuminated, and this can only take place when they

---

[19]Morris, *Corinthians*, p. 57.

[20]Ironside, *I Corinthians*, pp. 99-100.

[21]Further difference can be seen in the two different Greek words translated "knew" in this verse. The spirit of man knows (*oida*) itself innately, whereas the Spirit of God knows (*ginōskō*) the Father and the Son by personal fellowship and coexistence with the trinitarian oneness.

have received the Holy Spirit. The Spirit teaches from within a believer, not from without. The verb "received" may be viewed from a personal perspective (received at the moment of salvation, Rom. 8:9; Eph. 1:13) or from a dispensational stance (received on the day of Pentecost).[22]

To whom does "we" refer? Hodge wrote, "Here, the whole connection shows that the apostle is speaking of revelation and inspiration; and therefore *we* must mean *we apostles,* or Paul himself, and not we Christians."[23] Later, Paul did comment, "For I think that God hath set forth us the apostles last . . ." (4:9). Thus, the personal pronouns "we" and "us" could have a restrictive, technical meaning. If so, then Paul definitely meant the reception, the proclamation, and the writing of revealed divine truth. He thus was talking about the order in the production of the written Word of God. If the terms are universally applied to all believers, then all Christians can potentially understand all that God has revealed because the agent of revelation, the Holy Spirit, is now within them. In either case, Paul pointed out the necessity of receiving the Spirit in order to know.

There is a slight problem over the meaning of "the spirit of the world." Satan is called "the prince of this world" (John 12:31); thus, some would equate "the spirit of the world" with the Satanic spirit. However, in no place is Satan directly described as the spirit of this world. It is better to view the phrase as a reference to the spirit of human wisdom that marks this world (cf. 2:13).[24] The "freely given" things are identical to the prepared things (2:9) and the revealed, deep things of God (2:10).[25]

3. The Holy Spirit is essential in instruction (2:13)

Paul claimed to speak the very things that the Spirit had revealed. As expressed by the prophets and the apostles, speak-

---

[22]The latter is the position of Grosheide, *Corinthians,* p. 70.

[23]Charles Hodge, *Commentary on the First Epistle to the Corinthians,* p. 40.

[24]This is Hodge's view. Ibid.

[25]The participle phrase "the things that are freely given" (*ta charisthenta*) is based on the word for "grace" (*charis*). God's self-disclosure and man's understanding are not based on any merit in man.

ing and writing were synonymous (Acts 1:16; 28:25). Paul made two claims for his speaking: one negative and one positive. Words are conveyors of thought. The apostle asserted that the words employed in his speaking and writing were not taught by human wisdom but, rather, by the Holy Spirit. This is strong support for the verbal inspiration of the apostolic writings. The Holy Spirit revealed truths and taught (not dictated) the words which would correctly express those truths. If inspiration is not the direct teaching of this verse, then certainly the principle that underlies inspiration is here. Paul wrote what the Spirit taught; we believers today should likewise teach what the Spirit has taught us through the written Word.

The closing phrase ("comparing spiritual things with spiritual") is very difficult to interpret. Morris observed, "The solution is not easy, and a final decision perhaps impossible."[26] The problem is centered in the gender of the words, "comparing spiritual things [pneumatika; neuter] with spiritual [pneumatikois; masculine or neuter]." These possibilities exist: expounding spiritual truths to spiritually minded men; or comparing spiritual ideas with spiritual words; or comparing spiritual truths with other spiritual truths (one Bible passage with another); or communicating spiritual things by spiritual methods. The context seems to reflect Boyer's conclusion: ". . . making the utterance correspond to the thought, using Spirit-taught words to express Spirit-given truth."[27]

The emphasis, however, is clear. Revelation, inspiration, illumination, and instruction must be controlled by the Spirit of God. Apart from Him, the wisdom of God cannot be known.

II. RESPONSES TO DIVINE WISDOM (2:14 — 3:4)

Paul now moved from the objective nature of divine wisdom to the subjective responses to it. Therein was the heart of the Corinthian dilemma. Their membership was probably marked by three different types of men with the majority within the carnality grouping.

[26]Morris, *Corinthians*, p. 59.

[27]James L. Boyer, *For a World Like Ours*, p. 40.

A. Response by the Natural Man (2:14)

The words "natural man" refer to the unsaved man. Paul described him in five ways.

1. The natural man is soulish

He is soulish or psychical (based on the Greek word *psychikos*). Jude characterized him as "sensual [same word], having not the Spirit" (Jude v. 19). Within the immaterial part of man, a distinction is made between soul and spirit (I Thess. 5:23; Heb. 4:12). The natural man operates within the soul realm because he is spiritually dead (Eph. 2:1). Boyer asserted: "This word [*psychikos*] was first used by Aristotle to distinguish the pleasures of the soul, i.e., ambition and desire for knowledge, from those of the body, which were the grosser fleshly pleasures. Thus the word was used by Greek writers to distinguish the noblest of men."[28] In agreement, Morris added: "It refers to the man whose horizon is bounded by the things of this life. It is the worldly wise man again. . . ."[29]

2. The natural man does not receive spiritual things ("the things of the Spirit of God")

He totally and persistently does not welcome spiritual concepts. He is inhospitable to Biblical doctrines and moral principles. Believers are commanded to "receive with meekness the engrafted word, which is able to save [their] souls" (James 1:21). Jesus said, "He that is of God heareth God's words: ye therefore hear them not, because ye are not of God" (John 8:47).

3. The natural man regards spiritual things as foolishness

The reason why he rejects spiritual things is that he regards them as "foolishness" (cf. 1:18–25). To him, they are "absurd, insipid, and distasteful."[30]

[28]Ibid., p. 41.

[29]Morris, *Corinthians*, p. 60.

[30]Hodges, *Corinthians*, p. 43.

4. *The natural man has no spiritual ability*

He has no inner ability to know spiritual things. It is not that he will not know them, but rather that he "cannot know them."

5. *The natural man does not have the Holy Spirit*

The cause of his inability to know spiritual things is that they are spiritually discerned by men in whom the Spirit dwells and enlightens. The natural man does not have the Spirit; therefore, he has no capacity to receive spiritual things. The noun form of the verb "discerned" is used of a pretrial examination (Acts 25:26); thus, unbelievers are not even capable of giving a preliminary verdict about the nature of divine wisdom. Their need is to be saved and to receive the indwelling presence of the Holy Spirit.

B. Response by the Spiritual Man (2:15–16)

The second person, "he that is spiritual [*pneumatikos;* the plural form of this word was used in verse 13]," is saved, indwelt by the Spirit of God, and yielded to Him. No longer blinded by Satan (II Cor. 4:4), he has been enlightened by God (Eph. 1:18). He is spiritually alive, Spirit-controlled, and in a position to receive Biblical truths. Three qualities are ascribed to him.

1. *The spiritual man judges all things*

He judges, discerns, or examines (*anakrinō;* same verb as 2:14) all spiritual things. Grosheide wrote: "Not as if the spiritual man would have to state his opinion about everything. The implication is rather that he is able and permitted to judge. The spiritual man is not limited in his judging: everything he desires to judge he may judge."[31]

2. *The spiritual man is judged by no man*

He is judged (discerned or examined [same verb again]) by no unbeliever. Just as an unsaved person cannot know spiritual things because they are spiritually discerned, so he cannot understand the spiritual man's position, Biblical understanding, or Spirit-directed life.

[31]Grosheide, *Corinthians,* p. 74.

3. The spiritual man has the mind of Christ

The connective "for" introduces the reason why the spiritual man cannot be examined by the natural man. Zophar asked, "Canst thou by searching find out God?" (Job 11:7). Paul's answer, taken from the Old Testament (Isa. 40:13), is clear. Since no man knows the mind of God, no man can teach or counsel God; since all spiritual believers have the mind of Christ, no unsaved person can counsel them.

C. Response by the Carnal Man (3:1–4)

The third person mentioned by Paul is saved and indwelt by the Holy Spirit, but is not yielded to Him. He is identified in four ways.

1. The "carnal" man is saved

He is a brother, a member of the family of God through regeneration (John 1:12). However, he is not able to receive the same level of instruction as the spiritual Christian. Instead of manifesting the mind of Christ, he is reflecting the mind of natural man.

2. The carnal man is fleshly

He is carnal. There is a slight difference between the two Greek words translated as "carnal" in this section. He is carnal (sarkinos in 3:1) in that he has not gained the victory over his indwelling sin nature (cf. Rom. 7:14, same word). He is positionally justified, but there is no practical sanctification in his life. This condition marks many immature, unknowledgeable Christians. In addition, he is carnal (sarkikos in 3:3) in that he has willfully chosen to yield himself to the sin nature rather than to the Holy Spirit. A child of God does live in the flesh (Gal. 2:20), but he should not live according to the flesh (Rom. 8:12).

3. The carnal man is a babe

He must be treated as a babe (nēpios) in Christ. He is a Christian, but he is like a newborn infant, one who must be supported by others. His spiritual diet is limited. Like a baby, he can only receive "milk," not "meat." Biblical milk involves fundamental, theological principles (Heb. 5:12). Milk-users cannot apply Biblical passages to life situations (Heb. 5:13). They lack experience to discern between good and evil (Heb. 5:14). The carnality of the Corinthians was not new. They had not been able to digest meat in the past ("hitherto ye were not able"), and they are still not yet able to handle it ("neither yet now are ye able").

4. The carnal man acts like the unsaved man

His behavior is no different than that of unsaved men (3:3). When he manifests the attitudes and actions of envy, strife, and division (cf. 1:11), he walks according to the standards and life-style of man (*kata anthrōpon*). Carnality is expressed by following or exalting one Christian leader at the expense of others (3:4).

QUESTIONS FOR DISCUSSION

1. Should ministers study hermeneutics (the science of Biblical interpretation) and homiletics (the art of preaching), and literature to improve their sermonic presentations? Or should they depend solely on the guidance and inspiration of the Holy Spirit? Should you use commentaries and other Bible study aids? Or depend solely on the guidance of the Holy Spirit as you study the Bible?

2. How can a believer maintain the delicate balance between a sense of human insufficiency and a confidence in divine enablement?

3. What are some of the Biblical concepts that do not appear in non-Christian world religions?

4. How important is the doctrine of the divine inspiration of the Bible?

5. How can spirituality be gained and maintained?

6. What are the causes of carnality within evangelical churches? How can it be eliminated?

7. Does contemporary preaching primarily manifest the "milk" or the "meat" approach? Are both approaches necessary? What determines this?

3

The Role of the Minister
I Corinthians 3:5 — 4:21

The carnal divisiveness within the church was caused by following human leaders (1:12; cf. 3:4). In this lengthy section, Paul's solution to the problem continued. After pointing out the difference between divine and human wisdom, now the apostle wanted the Corinthians to have a proper concept of the ministers through whom the Spirit of God had taught them spiritual truth. In other passages, the servant of God is seen as a fisherman (Matt. 4:19), a bishop (I Tim. 3:1), an elder (Titus 1:5), a shepherd (I Peter 5:2), and a soldier (II Tim. 2:3); but here, Paul characterized him in five different ways: as a farmer, builder, steward, fool, and father.

I. A FARMER (3:5–9)

During His earthly ministry, Jesus Christ often used the imagery of agriculture (sowing the seed; wheat and tares; fields white unto harvest) to describe the relationship of the preaching of the gospel to men (Matt. 9:35–38; 13:1–30, 36–43). Paul now used this same analogy to point out the minister's relationships both to other servants and to God within the gospel ministry.

A. Man's Work

Two questions begin this paragraph: "Who [or what] then is Paul? and who [or what]¹ is Apollos?" Since the Corinthians had

¹The received text has the interrogative pronoun *tis* ("who"), whereas the critical text has *ti* ("what"). The former focuses on the identity of the two personalities, but the latter emphasizes their functions. The critical text also mentions Apollos before Paul.

exalted these two leaders, this was a natural inquiry. Five answers will be given concerning the roles of Paul and Apollos.

First, they were mere ministers (*diakonoi*). The word here does not signify the formal office of pastor or deacon. Just as Christ came not to be ministered unto, but to minister (Matt. 20:28), so Paul and Apollos did the same. Just as the ministers, or table waiters (John 2:5), served by giving wine to the guests at the marriage feast of Cana, so Paul served by giving out the gospel to men and women throughout the world (Col. 1:23, 25).

Second, both Paul and Apollos were instruments or channels by or through (*dia*) whom the Corinthians had believed in Christ. Faith was not placed *in* them or *because* of them. Faith is the gift of God which comes through hearing the Word of God (Rom. 10:17; Eph. 2:8–9), but ". . . how shall they believe in him of whom they have not heard? and how shall they hear without a preacher? And how shall they preach, except they be sent?" (Rom. 10:14–15). Paul and Apollos were commissioned, obedient preachers.

A threshing floor near Konya (ancient Iconium).

Third, they had planted and watered the Word of God in Corinth (13:6). Paul originally evangelized the city (Acts 18:1–18), whereas Apollos preached in Corinth later (Acts 18:24 — 19:1). Although Apollos and Paul had different ministries at different times, Paul pointed out that they shared the same purpose (3:8a). They wanted to see increase and to have God glorified by their effort.

Fourth, ministers will receive a reward or wages for work accomplished based upon their individual[2] effort or toil expended in their labor (3:8b), not upon their abilities or success. Fifth, both Paul and Apollos were fellow-workers ("labourers together") with one another and with God.[3]

B. God's Work

The interrelationship of God and man in the ministry can clearly be seen in this passage (cf. John 15:26–27). First, God is responsible for giving converts to each minister (3:5b); thus, spiritual children are gifts, not wages. Second, only God can give spiritual "increase" (3:6). Only He can germinate life within a dead sinner and nourish that regenerated soul.[4] Compared to God, the source and sustainer of life, man's ministry at its very best is still insignificant (3:7). Third, God alone is responsible for giving wages to each laborer (3:8). Fourth, God saves, employs, and works with each minister (note use of "we," 3:9a). Fifth, the church belonged to God, not to any man (note use of "ye" 3:9b). It is *His* farm or garden, and it is *His* building.[5] Christ said that He would build His church (Matt. 16:18). He owns it and He is building it.

---

[2]Note the emphasis upon individuality in this passage: "every man" (*hekastos,* 3:5, 8, 10, 13 [twice]) and "his own" (*idion,* 3:8 [twice]).

[3]The Greek word order puts the emphasis on God. "*God's* fellow-workers we are."

[4]The verbs indicate that human activities begin and end, but God keeps on doing His work. "Planted" and "watered" are aorists, whereas "gave the increase" is imperfect and "giveth the increase" is present.

[5]The Greek word order emphasizes God's ownership. The word *theou* occurs both before "husbandry" and "building."

II. A BUILDER (3:10–23)

By mentioning the metaphors of farming and building in the same verse (3:9), Paul formed a fitting transition from the minister's role as a farmer to that of a builder.

A. The Master Builder (3:10–11)

Paul regarded himself as the "master builder" or architect (*architektōn*). Christ had revealed to him the blueprint for the church (Eph. 2:19 — 3:12), and thus as an apostle, Paul had the responsibility to serve as the general contractor, laying the foundation and superintending the spiritual construction by his associates and by the believers (4:17; cf. Eph. 2:20). He was "wise" in that his skill was imparted to him by the grace of God through the Holy Spirit (cf. the workmen who erected and adorned the tabernacle; Exod. 35:10, 25; 36:1, 4, 8). Paul knew that both his position and abilities were gifts of God's grace; in himself he had no basis for boasting. He claimed that he had not only laid the foundation of the Corinthian church with his pioneer evangelistic work, but that no other foundation could be laid upon or beside[6] his. He had done his job accurately and completely. The foundation of the true church consists only of the person and redemptive work of Jesus Christ (Matt. 16:15–21; Eph. 2:20; I Peter 2:6). It involves the proper recognition of the fact that Christ is both God and man, and of the acceptance of His death, burial, and resurrection as the basis of divine forgiveness.

B. The After-Builders (3:12–23)

Paul knew that others would build a superstructure upon his ministry, but this is different from building another foundation. He wanted them to watch out *how* they built (3:10). It must be according to the plans of the architect and in proper relationship to the foundation cornerstone of Christ.

1. The materials (3:12)

The type of construction ("how") is based on the choice of building materials. What are they? In ancient times, the "gold,"

---

[6]The phrase "than that is laid" literally reads "beside that which is laid," based upon the preposition *para*.

The Parthenon at Athens.

"silver," and "precious stones" referred to the costly ornamentation which adorned pagan temples and royal palaces (cf. Rev. 21:18–19). However, the stones may refer to the use of granite or marble subsequently adorned with gold and silver (cf. I Kings 7:9–11). In lesser construction, "wood" was used for the doors and posts, "hay" was dried grass mixed with mud for making walls, and "stubble" was the straw used for the roof. The evident contrast is in value and permanence. But what spiritual building materials do these items represent? Since the foundation is a person, then the materials must also be persons (I Peter 2:6). The issue is clear. What kind of people are you building through your ministry? Are value and permanence being created within lives affected by your teaching of doctrinal and moral truths? The materials thus manifest the quality of the ministry of the after-builders as seen in the lives of their converts. Although the passage has a primary interpretation and application to the professional ministry,[7] in principle it can also refer to any believer who has an influence on others.

2. The inspection (3:13–15)

Just as houses must meet the building codes of cities, so spiritual work must, and will, be evaluated. The answers to these questions will be made manifest then: What did he do? How did he do it? Why did he do it? The Day of Judgment, the event that immediately follows Christ's return (4:5; cf. II Cor. 5:10), will show forth the quality of each man's ministry. In the metaphor of testing the permanence of building materials, Paul asserted that the work "shall be revealed by fire."[8] The fire is designed neither to punish the person nor to refine the believer or his work, but to unmask the essence of his Christian effort (to show it like it really is). It will test the work to determine its quality ("sort"), not its quantity ("how much").

The results of the test are either positive or negative. Abiding work (gold, silver, precious stones) will bring a reward to the worker (3:14). These rewards are also called crowns: an incorruptible crown for living the disciplined life (9:25); a crown of rejoicing for successful witnessing (I Thess. 2:19); a crown of righteousness for loving Christ's appearing (II Tim. 4:8); a crown of life for enduring trials (James 1:12); and a crown of glory for faithful pastors (I Peter 5:4). Worthless, temporary effort (wood, hay, stubble) will be "burned" (3:15) — consumed. The believer will suffer the loss of reward, but not of salvation ("he . . . shall be saved"). His practice will be tested, not his position. His spiritual standing is secure because his wasted life still rested upon the foundation of Christ's redemptive work. The fire serves as the trial, not as a punishment for sin after the trial.

3. The warning (3:16–23)

Three basic warnings are given. The first warning is clear: Do not "defile the temple of God" (3:16–17). To avoid this sin,

[7]See Charles Hodge, *Commentary on the First Epistle to the Corinthians*, p. 56; James L. Boyer, *For a World Like Ours*, pp. 49-50; A Robertson and A. Plummer, *I Corinthians*, p. 62.

[8]There is a slight grammatical problem over the subject of the verb. The word "it" could refer either to the day or the work.

Paul wanted his readers to realize three truths: (1) corporately they were the temple of God, (2) the Spirit of God was dwelling in their midst, and (3) they were holy. The temple of God thus is composed of believers individually indwelt by the Holy Spirit, joined together by their common faith in Christ and founded upon His redemptive work (cf. Eph. 2:19–22). This word for "temple" (*naos*) refers to the inner sanctuary of God's presence, whereas the other word (*hieron*) included all of the temple property. The words "defile" and "destroy" are actually derived from the same Greek verb (*phtheirō*). Thus, punishment is in kind (Gal. 6:7).

To whom was the warning given? Some believe that the defilers are unsaved, false teachers within the church contrasted with the saved, faulty teachers (cf. 3:15).[9] To defile means to waste, to damage, to corrupt, or to deprave. For the defilement of the tabernacle, Jews received death (Lev. 15:31). Thus, the judgment of God could refer to the chastisement of physical death (cf. 11:30). The context seems to favor a warning against saved teachers.

In his second warning Paul returned to the problem of the Christian's attraction to worldly wisdom (cf. 1:18–25): Do not exalt self and human wisdom (3:18–20). This admonition is grammatically based upon two imperatives: "Let no man deceive himself" and "Let him become a fool" (3:18). The logic behind the warning is piercing. To elevate one's self is self-deception; thus, to abase self is the key to becoming spiritually wise. Those who are impressed with their own wisdom must repudiate that wisdom and must recognize their spiritual ignorance in order to be taught the wisdom of God. For proof, Paul cited two Old Testament passages (3:19b–20; cf. Job 5:13; Ps. 94:11) to demonstrate that both the methods and the reasonings of the worldly wise are vain or fruitless before God.

The third warning is based upon the imperative, "Therefore let no man glory in men" (3:21). It is actually the result of the former admonition ("therefore" [*hōste*] introduces a Greek result clause). The reason for the warning is introduced by the

---

[9]This position is held by Boyer, *World Like Ours*, p. 52; Leon Morris, *The First Epistle of Paul to the Corinthians*, p. 70; and S. Lewis Johnson, "First Corinthians," *The Wycliffe Bible Commentary*, p. 1235.

explanatory word "for." The general statement ("all things are yours") is then broken down into specifics (3:22). To "glory in men" is a failure to recognize that all gifted preachers and teachers are given for the mutual blessing of all of God's people. In addition, the material world created and sustained by God, the nature of life and death, and the circumstances of time are all the divinely imparted possessions of each believer (cf. Rom. 8:38–39). The sequence of possession or belonging (3:22b–23) is designed to show that no believer has an exclusive claim to truth and also that no believer should feel left out. All things belong to believers; all believers belong to Christ; Christ belongs to God — thus, all believers belong to God.

III. A STEWARD (4:1–5)

Stewardship over the goods and house of the master by a devoted servant was part of the ancient culture (Gen. 15:2; 43:19; 44:4; II Chron. 28:1). Jesus Christ used that analogy to depict proper Christian service and responsibility (Matt. 20:8; Luke 12:42; 16:1–8). Paul now identified the minister in this fashion.

A. His Characteristics (4:1–2)

Paul wanted Apollos and himself to be known ("Let a man so account of us") by the church in three areas.

1. A minister

Paul wanted to be recognized as the "minister of Christ." This is not the typical word for minister (*diakonos*), but rather *hypēretas*, literally meaning "under-rower." It was used of the slave who rowed in the lower bank of oars on a large ancient ship. Subsequently, it came to refer to any subordinate — usually an assistant, a helper, or a synagogue attendant (Luke 4:20). It was used of John Mark (Acts 13:5), of other gospel preachers (Luke 1:2), of Paul's associates (Acts 24:23), and of Paul himself (Acts 20:34; 26:16). Paul, thus, did not see himself as a man of high spiritual status, but rather as Christ's assistant, a helper willing to do the lowest task.

CALLED TO BE SAINTS

2. A steward

Paul wanted to be known as a "steward [*oikonomos*] of the
mysteries of God." The word for *steward* literally means "house
law." A steward was an administrator, a trustee, an overseer of
an estate. He was under the owner and over others within the
house. Both Paul and Peter (I Peter 4:10) knew that God had
assigned to them an awesome responsibility over the church and
the revealed truths of the New Testament. As a minister, Paul
was to serve and to do; as a steward, he was to protect and to
guide.

3. A faithful man

Paul wanted to be known as a faithful steward. Faithfulness
involves doing all that the master has commanded, doing it according to the master's method, and doing it in the assigned
time. The sphere of stewardship may vary but the quality never
does: "For unto whomsoever much is given, of him shall be
much required; and to whom men have committed much, of
him they will ask the more" (Luke 12:48).

B. His Judgment (4:3–5)

The preceding verse (4:2) used two key verbs: "required"
and "be found." But who determines whether a steward has
been faithful? Three options are offered.

1. By others (4:3a)

Paul had earlier said that the spiritual man is not judged by
anyone (2:15). The same verb (*anakrinō*) is used here. Paul knew
that the approval or disapproval of his stewardship did not rest
upon their acceptance or rejection of his ministry. They had not
commissioned him; therefore, he was not accountable to them.
He was not bothered by the fact that they did attempt to evaluate
his ministry and that they compared him to others. The two
prepositional phrases refer to the subjective criteria of judgment
by believers ("of you") and by the world's standards ("of man's
judgment"; literally, "by man's day"). Success by the world is
viewed outwardly and quantitatively.

52

2. By himself (4:3b–4a)

Paul also knew that he was not capable of judging his own ministry. He clearly stated that he did not try to appraise his stewardship objectively, subjectively, or comparatively. As far as he knew, he did not detect any flaw in his ministry ("I know nothing by [literally, against] myself"). He believed that he was doing what God commanded and that his motivations were correct. However, he would not base the success or divine acceptance of his stewardship upon his clear conscience ("yet am I not hereby justified"). Paul knew the truth of Solomon's counsel: "Every way of a man is right in his own eyes: but the Lord pondereth the hearts" (Prov. 21:2).

3. By Christ (4:4b–5)

Paul knew, nevertheless, that both his ministry and he were under constant, divine scrutiny.[10] At other times, he had appealed to God as an examiner and a witness to his integrity (I Thess. 2:4–5, 10). Here too he says, "He that judgeth me is the Lord." Since Christ was already judging him, Paul appealed to his readers to stop judging anything about his ministry or that of others. That was not their task (cf. Rom. 14:10, 13).

Preliminary ("before the time") human judgments are invalid. When Christ returns, an accurate assessment of men, methods, and motivations will take place. Two basic facts, unobtainable by outward human observation, will then be disclosed. First, Christ "will bring to light the hidden things of darkness." This probably refers to deeds done when a person is alone, totally unsupervised or watched by men. Second, He "will make manifest the counsels of the hearts." This refers to the reasons why ministers did what they did. Were they selfish or altruistic, anthropocentric or theocentric? The result of this final judgment is that "the praise shall come to each one from God" (literal translation). The classic statement that Paul wanted to hear was, "Well done, good and faithful servant" (Matt. 24:21, 23). This phrase is for a completed task ("done"), quality work ("well"), constant effort ("faithful"), and personal integrity ("good"). There is a slight problem with the word *hekastōi* ("every man").

---

[10]Note the use of the present tense rather than the future.

Does it refer to every believer, or to every faithful worker? Is there a difference between praise and reward (3:14)?

IV. A PARADOX (4:6–13)

The basic problem that produced the Corinthian divisions was pride in self and in others. Paul wanted to show them that their opinions of themselves and of him were just the opposite of his. Until they saw themselves as they really were before God and men, they could not have a spirit of genuine spiritual unity.

A. In Principle (4:6–7)

1. No Christian is better than another (4:6)

Paul used the names of Apollos and himself (cf. 1:12; 3:4, 22) instead of the names of the schismatic leaders in Corinth in order to deal with the problem on the basis of principle, not of personality. The word "transferred" (*meteschēmatisa*; cf. II Cor. 11:15) means to change the outward appearance or identity. He chose this method "for your sakes." If he had mentioned the leaders by name, the church would have been further divided. Men like Paul, Apollos, and Cephas were above such petty differences; therefore, they were used for the object lesson ("that ye might learn *in us*"). There were two purposes behind the transfer (each introduced by "that"). Men should not elevate other Christians beyond the Scriptural positioning of men (cf. Jer. 9:23–24). Also, men should not exalt themselves at the expense of others. The sandlot baseball concept of choosing up sides should not be followed by humble Christians.

2. Every Christian is indebted to God (4:7)

Every believer should recognize that he has received his ability and influence from God. Three direct questions are asked to emphasize this concept. Hodge commented on the first question thus: "Who thinks you are better than others? Your superiority over your brethren is mere self-conceit and inflation. The difference between you is only imaginary."[11] The second question points out that God is the real source of differences (personalities, abilities, appearance). The third question shows the

---

[11]Hodge, *Corinthians*, pp. 70-71.

folly of glorying in self when the object of false glory is a gift that has actually come from God, the one who really deserves the glory.

B. In Practice (4:8–13)

Attitude leads to actions. In behavior, Paul noted a sharp contrast between that of the Corinthians and that of himself. Their reception by the world was far different from that which he received.

1. Contrast between Paul and the church (4:8-10)

With inspired sarcasm, he used three statements[12] to repudiate their faulty evaluation of themselves (4:8). There is a decided progression in the criticism: "full" — "rich" — "kings." Fullness represents self-satisfaction (cf. Acts 27:38; "eaten enough" is the same word). Riches portray self-sufficiency. They manifested the Laodicean spirit: "Because thou sayest, I am rich, and increased with goods, and have need of nothing; and knowest not that thou art wretched, and miserable, and poor, and blind, and naked" (Rev. 3:17). Kingship revealed a sense of spiritual triumph with no more conflict. This will only take place in the millennial kingdom. This is why Paul ironically added "and I would to God ye did reign, that we also might reign with you." Paul was still fighting a spiritual warfare, but the Corinthian Christians, in their opinion, felt they had arrived at spiritual maturity (cf. Phil. 3:12-14).

In contrast to the Corinthians' high opinion of themselves, Paul and the apostles looked like failures (4:9). The church had promoted itself to first place ("kings"), but God "had set forth the apostles last." The verb "set forth" was used of doomed gladiators forced into the arenas to fight and to die. The church expected to live, but Paul knew that the apostles were appointed to martyrdom, like condemned criminals (Rom. 8:36; II Cor. 11:23–30). At Ephesus, where Paul wrote this letter, this is what almost happened to his associates (Acts 19:23, 29). They were also made a spectacle (the English "theater" is the transliteration

---

[12]Some see these as questions: Are you already full? Have you already become rich? Apart from us did you begin to reign?

CALLED TO BE SAINTS

of the Greek *theatron*) to the world of evil angels and unsaved men.[13] This concept was used of conquered peoples paraded before the public as objects of derision (cf. Heb. 11:33–40).

In a series of three contrasts (4:10), Paul pointed out the differences mentally ("fools" vs. "wise"), physically ("weak" vs. "strong"), and socially ("honourable" vs. "despised").[14] Before the world, Paul viewed himself and the apostles as nothing, yet the Corinthians prided themselves on their acceptance in the world.

2. Contrast between Paul and the world (4:11–13)

Paul began and ended this section with similar expressions of time ("unto this present hour . . . unto this day"). Persecution had marked the apostle's life from the time of his conversion (Acts 9:23) to his present ministry at Ephesus (16:9). It was not incidental, but constant; and yet the Corinthians had not suffered for their faith. In a series of six verbs (4:11–12a) he pointed out his mistreated position in the world. Then in a series of three participles and three verbs (4:12b–13a) he expressed his spiritual reaction to the persecution. He blessed those who reviled him with injurious words (cf. I Peter 2:23), suffered, or put up with, those who physically harmed him, and exhorted those who defamed or attacked his character by ascribing evil deeds and motives to his ministry. In conclusion, he knew that the world viewed the apostles as filth and offscouring. The word "filth" (*perikatharmata*) refers to the sweepings and dust from the floor, the rinsings of dirty pans; "offscourings" (*peripsēma*) involves the food particles wiped off dishes and pots by rubbing hard. They were regarded as nothing but dust and garbage!

V. A FATHER (4:14–21)

Paul ended by reminding the Corinthians that he was more than a typical minister to them because he was their spiritual father. Thus, his relationship was far more intimate than those who discredited his ministry.

[13]The literal translation is "to the world both angels and men." There is an article before "world," but not before the other two.

[14]Note the slight change of order: "We . . . ye; We . . . ye; Ye . . . we."

A. In Conception (4:14–16)

Paul approached them as any father would in correcting an erring son. The first four chapters were not designed to shame or embarrass the Corinthians. No father wants to ridicule his children publicly or provoke them to anger (Eph. 6:4). Rather, to demonstrate that he still loved them, Paul had to warn them (cf. Eph. 6:4, same word translated "admonition"). He had to speak frankly; he could not remain silent or indifferent.

Many teachers do not replace one parent (4:15). In the ancient educational system, instructors (*paidagōgoi*) usually were slaves with no personal attachment to their students (cf. Gal. 3:24–25; 4:1–3). In the church, the believers had been subjected to various ministers since their conversion, but they needed to remember that it was Paul, and only he, who was the human instrument in their new birth (cf. Philem. v. 10). Both God and man labor together to conceive and to beget believing sinners into the family of God. Thus, as obedient children, they should "be followers" (14:16; "follow," or "mimic" is based upon the Greek *mimētai*) of their father, namely Paul, in spiritual things.

B. In Instruction (4:17)

Paul wanted to go to Corinth to deal with the situation, but his ministry at Ephesus prevented him from doing so (16:3–9). So he sent Timothy as his authoritative representative. The sending of Timothy actually preceded the writing of the letter, although Paul knew that the letter would arrive in Corinth before Timothy.[15] Both Timothy and the believers were "beloved sons" of Paul (4:14; cf. 4:17); therefore, they had something in common. In addition, Timothy was a spiritually faithful person. Just as Timothy had received instruction from his spiritual father, Paul planned that his young associate would remind the Corinthians of his teaching which was communicated in every church. Paul did not treat them any differently than he would any other church.

---

[15]Some view the verb "have I sent" as an epistolary aorist. This means that the sending of Timothy by Paul was in the past at the time the Corinthians received the letter. However, since he is not mentioned in the salutation (1:1) and since Paul later speculated about his coming (14:10, "now *if* Timotheus come") it is better to conclude that Paul sent Timothy to Corinth by way of Macedonia.

C. In Correction (4:18–21)

Within the church was an emerging group which resisted
Paul's apostolic authority (9: 1–3; II Cor. 1:17; 10:10; 12:12). The
fact that Paul chose not to come personally just caused their egos
to be puffed up (4:18). They thought that the sending of both
Timothy and the letter demonstrated that Paul was afraid to face
them personally. However, Paul planned to visit the church at a
later time, *if* the trip was within the Lord's will. He then would
confront the arrogant dissidents with some basic spiritual concepts. Would their lives match their profession? Would they have
spiritual power, or would they be full of weak words (cf. Luke
11:20; Rom. 14:17)? They were as those "having a form of god-
liness, but denying the power thereof" (II Tim. 3:5).

Paul then placed the attitude of his next visit squarely before
them ("what will ye?"). Their response to the letter and to
Timothy's ministry would determine whether he would come in
full demonstration of his apostolic authority in correction and
discipline, or in the tender expression of a loving father. Disobedience would bring the rod of chastisement, but submission
and repentance would produce warm embraces.

QUESTIONS FOR DISCUSSION

1. What contemporary ministries could be called planting
and watering? Why are there often conflicts between them?

2. Are soul-winners exalted more than they should be? Is
lack of soul-winning a sign of spiritual failure?

3. Upon what bases are modern churches generally compared with each other? Evaluate these comparisons in the light
of the judgment seat of Christ.

4. In present evangelical circles, what would represent
"wood, hay, and stubble"? "Gold, silver, and precious stones"?

5. Why do Christians too often glory in men? What can be
done to discourage this sin?

6. Are affluent Christians more likely to be like the carnal
Corinthians than like the despised apostles? If so, what can be
done to correct the dilemma?

7. How straightforward should a Christian be when he attempts to correct an erring brother? What approaches should he use to effect a reconciliation?

4

Fornication and Church Discipline

I Corinthians 5

False thinking leads to false living. The exaltation of worldly wisdom in Corinth naturally fostered a worldly attitude toward sin among its members. Paul recognized that the problems in the church were not just mental or intellectual, but they were also moral and spiritual. In its letter of inquiry (7:1), the church asked about the issues of marriage, Christian liberty, the position of women, spiritual gifts, and the resurrection of the dead; but it failed to reveal its sins of division (chaps. 1 — 14), sexual abuse (chap. 5), lack of discipline (chap. 5), and lawsuits between members (chap. 6). After attempting to solve the problem of church division, Paul now moved to their tolerant attitude toward a terrible act of sin.

I. THE ACT OF SIN (5:1)

The transition between the two chapters seems rather abrupt, but there is some indication of continuity. The rod of apostolic discipline (4:21) can be applied to both dissensions and moral sin (5:3–5). The pride of resistance to authority can be seen in both sections ("puffed up," 4:18–19; cf. 5:2). To follow Paul (4:16) means to share in his treatment of the sinner (5:4).

A. It Was Well Known

Paul's report was not based upon rumor but upon fact. The adverb "commonly" (*holōs*) means "altogether" or "actually" (translated "utterly" in 6:7). The apostle never would have given this direct counsel if the report had simply been based upon suspicion. In a divided church, it would have been very easy to start rumors about the opposition; but in this situation, all parties were in agreement over the actual occurrence of the sin. The text literally reads "it is being heard" (*akouetai*). No doubt Paul heard about the sin from both the household of Chloe (1:11) and the three church messengers (16:17). The prepositional phrase "among you" may mean that the report was only being circulated within the church and that the unsaved Corinthians had not yet heard of it. Or, it may mean that both the churches and the unsaved had heard about the presence of immorality within their assembly. In either case, the sin was no longer a secret, but known in enough circles to destroy the church's reputation.

B. It Was Fornication

The sin was "fornication" (*porneia;* "pornography" comes from this word). The noun is based upon two verbs (*peraō* and *pernēmi*) which convey the idea of selling bodies, both male and female, for lustful purposes. It developed into a general word for sexual immorality, both within and without the marital union. Some of the Corinthians had been saved out of a life of fornication (6:9; cf. 6:11), but that lustful tendency was still present within the church (6:13–20). To have a known fornicator within the church was bad enough, but his sexual perversion was of a type not normally committed even by the pagan Gentiles, nor condoned by them. Since the Roman world was known for its immorality (Rom. 1:24–32), that was quite an accusation.

C. It Was Specific

The sin specifically involved a man living sexually with his father's wife. The verb "have" (*echein*) means that they were living together as legal or common-law marital partners (cf. John 4:18). It does not imply that they had only one illicit affair together. This type of relationship was severely condemned by God in the Mosaic law (Lev. 18:8; Deut. 22:30). There is a slight problem over the meaning of "his father's wife" (literally, "a wife of the father"). Although it could possibly refer to the man's natural mother, that is unlikely since Paul could have used the term "mother" if that had been his meaning. Rather, it no doubt refers to the stepmother. Some unknowns, however, still remain. Was the father dead? Were the father and stepmother divorced? Did he seduce her while his father and she were still married?

II. THE ATTITUDE OF THE CHURCH (5:2)

A. Pride

Paul was aghast, but the church was apathetic. He cried: "And ye are puffed up. . . ." They had swelled heads instead of broken hearts. The verbal phrase indicates a constant state of pride.[1] The personal pronoun "ye" is emphatic, showing that all of the dissenting parties were guilty of this sin. Their pride (4:6, 18–19) persisted in spite of the presence of immorality in their midst. In fact, they were proud of their toleration. They were so preoccupied with themselves that no sin could move them out of their self-complacency.

B. Lack of Mourning

Rather, they should have mourned over this sinning brother as if they were lamenting the death of a loved one. The statement may very well be a question: "Should you not rather have mourned?" The presence of the negative "not" (ouchi) in the phrase implies an affirmative answer. They needed to obey the admonition: "Be afflicted, and mourn, and weep: let your laughter be turned to mourning, and your joy to heaviness. Humble yourselves in the sight of the Lord, and he shall lift you up" (James 4:9–10). Genuine mourning over the presence of sin brings the blessing of God (Matt. 5:4).

C. Lack of Discipline

The conjunction "that" (hina) introduces the purpose for the mourning. Mourning, for its own sake, is not healthy; it must lead to action. The verb, in the emphatic position (appearing first in the clause), means that the church should not expect the sinner to withdraw gradually from the fellowship of the church, but rather they should initiate the action of lifting him out of their midst. We may conclude that discipline is to be exercised

[1]The phrase is based upon the perfect passive participle in a periphrastic construction (pephusiōmenoi este). They were like a balloon that had been blown up and kept in that state.

only upon the man ("he that hath done," *ho poiēsas),* and not upon the woman. This would seem to indicate that the wife of the father was not a professing believer within the church. This would compound the sin of the professing member because he not only committed the act of immorality but he chose to live with an unsaved woman. Thus, his basis for union was lust and not love founded upon spiritual principles.

III. THE ATTITUDE OF PAUL (5:3–5)

Morris aptly commented: "Those who were present and might have been expected to have taken action had done nothing. He who was absent, and might have pleaded distance as an excuse for inaction, was not to be deterred from taking strong measures."[2] The contrasts between the two attitudes will be self-evident. In grammatical construction, these three verses actually form one lengthy sentence.

A. He Had Judged the Man (5:3)

Paul was unable to be physically present. His work at Ephesus prevented him from going to Corinth at this time (16:7–9). However, geographical absence did not mean noninvolvement. He constantly prayed for and communicated with distant believers and churches (Col. 2:1, 5; I Thess. 2:17). Although he was "absent in body" he was "present in spirit"; thus he was personally, spiritually, and directly involved. He had a right to express himself and to act.

The verb "have judged" (*kekrika*) shows that Paul had reached an unalterable decision about the offender. The facts reported to him provided sufficient evidence upon which to base a firm verdict. In fact, his judgment reflected the observation of an eyewitness ("as though I were present"). Again, his judgment was directed only at the man ("him"). The initial action of adultery ("hath done") was basis enough for church discipline, let alone living together. The adverb "so" (cf. John 3:16) reinforces the type of sin not acceptable even in pagan society.

B. He Desired a Unified Authority (5:4)

Because the sentence is long, there is a slight problem with

[2]Leon Morris, *The First Epistle of Paul to the Corinthians,* p. 87.

the relationship of the prepositional phrase "in the name of our Lord Jesus Christ." Grammatically, it could go with any of these three verbal concepts: "I have judged,"[3] "when ye are gathered together," or "to deliver."[4] Regardless, only the authority of the exalted head of the church (Matt. 16:18; Eph. 1:22) provides the justification for apostolic decisions, for the gathering of believers within local churches, and for the exercise of church discipline. The unified authority that Paul wanted involved three parties.

1. The authority included the local church

It included the local church ("when ye are gathered together"). This could refer to the regular meeting of the church or to a special public meeting called together for the sole purpose of exercising discipline. Since the local church is "the pillar and ground of the truth" (I Tim. 3:15), it must corporately deal with its sinning members. In a church marked by division, Paul did not want any group (e.g., Pauline party, Apollos group) or individual (pastor) to act alone.

2. The authority included Paul

It included Paul ("my spirit"). As an apostolic master builder commissioned directly by Christ, Paul had the right to speak authoritatively to the churches (II Thess. 3:14–15). This was a demonstration of his episcopal, shepherding ministry (II Cor. 11:28). In his physical absence, they would have the testimony of his authoritative, inspired epistle.

3. The authority included Christ

It included the authority of Christ Himself ("with the power of our Lord Jesus Christ").[5] The Lord clearly outlined the procedure of discipline:

Moreover if thy brother shall trespass against thee, go and tell

[3]Author's view. Also held by Charles Hodge, *Commentary on the First Epistle to the Corinthians,* p. 84.

[4]Morris, *Corinthians,* p. 87.

[5]This phrase could grammatically go with either "to deliver" or "when ye are gathered together." It probably goes with the latter. See Morris, ibid.

him his fault between thee and him alone: if he shall hear thee, thou hast gained thy brother.

But if he will not hear thee, then take with thee one or two more, that in the mouth of two or three witnesses every word may be established.

And if he shall neglect to hear them, tell it unto the church: but if he neglect to hear the church, let him be unto thee as an heathen man and a publican.

Verily I say unto you, whatsoever ye shall bind on earth shall be bound in heaven: and whatsoever ye shall loose on earth shall be loosed in heaven.

Again I say unto you, that if two of you shall agree on earth as touching anything that they shall ask, it shall be done for them of my Father which is in heaven.

For where two or three are gathered together in my name, there am I in the midst of them.   Matthew 18:15–20

Thus the local church not only has the divinely given right to discipline sinning members, but it is commanded to do so (II Thess. 3:6–15; Titus 3:10). The subsequent command to excommunicate implies that the church had already attempted to reconcile the erring brother but had failed.

C. He Wanted the Sinner Disciplined (5:5)

1. Statement of discipline

The essence of these three verses can be seen in this sequence: "I have judged . . . in the name of our Lord Jesus Christ . . . to deliver such an one unto Satan . . ." (5:3–5). God delivered Job to Satan for testing (Job 1:12; 2:6). Satan even asks for permission from God to try Christians (Luke 22:31). In the only other passage where this unique concept occurs, Paul delivered Hymenaeus and Alexander "unto Satan, that they may learn not to blaspheme" (I Tim. 1:20). Such a deliverance does not involve a consignment to Hades or the lake of fire or a loss of salvation. Rather, it is done for the believer's spiritual benefit. Outside the church is the world, the sphere of Satan's dominion (Eph. 2:12; Col. 1:13; I John 5:19). It is in that realm that Paul wanted to see the immoral Christian chastised. In essence, he called for excommunication and the withdrawal of all local church privileges. This radical step of deliverance to Satan was an apostolic prerogative, not given to any church or to any other individual. The powers of binding and loosing (Matt. 16:19) and of the remission and retention of sins (John 20:23) were given only to the apostles and very seldom were used by them (Acts 5:1–10; 13:8–11).

2. Purposes of discipline

There were two major purposes for the deliverance: "the destruction of the flesh" and "the salvation of the spirit." The second occurs only after the first has been achieved.[6] It is the flesh (*sarx*) which is destroyed, not the body. The flesh refers to the lusts of the sin nature (Gal. 5:16–21). This is what the offender needed to crucify (Gal. 5:24) to be restored to fellowship with God and with the church. Some see in this destruction the impartation of physical sickness and death (cf. 11:30).[7] Of course, God may permit Satan to afflict the body to get at the real cause of the problem, the dominant sin nature. Since the deliverance and the destruction result in the salvation of the spirit, the person must be regarded as a genuine believer in spite of his terrible sin.[8]

IV. THE APPEAL OF PAUL (5:6–13)

An attitude must manifest itself in action. After Paul had disclosed the attitudes of both the church and himself toward the sin, he now admonished the church to take definite action.

A. Do Not Glory (5:6)

Their glorying was absolutely not good.[9] The noun ("glory-

---

[6]The *hina* purpose clause (introduced by "that") grammatically develops out of *eis* purpose phrase (introduced by "for").

[7]Morris, *Corinthians*, p. 88.

[8]However, Boyer thinks that the reference is to an unsaved person, marked by insincerity and falseness (5:8) and mere profession (5:11), who repents and turns to Christ after recognizing the folly of his sin and the value of the Christian position. James L. Boyer, *For a World Like Ours*, p. 62.

[9]The adjective is very emphatic. The literal translation is: "Not good your glorying."

ing") refers to the matter of boasting — not to the act. But *what* they boasted about was not right. Morris observed: "It shows that the Corinthians did more than merely acquiesce in the situation. They were proud of their attitude."[10] To prove that statement, Paul appealed to their common sense: "Know ye not that a little leaven leaveneth the whole lump?" They gloried in their wisdom, and yet, they did not know this simple truth. To the Galatians, he pointed out that the false doctrines of the Judaizers would eventually corrupt the entire church if not removed (Gal. 5:9). Here, the toleration of evil would likewise spread and pollute all of them. Just as one rotten apple in a barrel of good apples will spoil them all, so undisciplined sinning members of the church will infect the entire group. And it doesn't take much tolerated sin to start the process!

B. Purge Out the Leaven (5:7)

1. The command

The command to purge conveys a decisive, thorough cleansing.[11] For a cancer operation to be successful, all of the cancerous cells must be removed; none can remain, or else the sick condition will be reintroduced. To purge means to withdraw fellowship (II Thess. 3:6, 14). The purpose for the discipline (indicated by "that") is that the church might return to a morally pure state ("new lump"), which they had lost through their dissensions and toleration of public sin. The reason or justification for the purge is seen in the clause "as [because] ye are unleavened." It is not that they will be unleavened if they do so, or that they ought to be unleavened. They are unleavened! This refers to their spiritual position or standing before God. In Christ, they were righteous, sanctified, and accepted. Now Paul wanted them to put their position into practice.

2. The reason

The reason for the purge is shown by the explanatory connective "for." According to the Mosaic regulations for the observance of the Passover and the Feast of Unleavened Bread (Exod.

[10]Morris, *Corinthians*, p. 89.

[11]The verb *ekkatharate* has the preposition *ek* prefix. The *ek* is used throughout this passage: "from," 5:2; "away," 5:13; and "from among," 5:13.

12:15; 13:7), no leavened bread was to be eaten at that time. The removal of leaven from the house took place before the feast. The applications to the Christian life are clear. Christ not only died during the Passover observance, but He was God's passover lamb who took away the sin of the world (John 1:29; I Peter 1:18–19). His substitutionary death removed our sin and imputed to us His righteousness (II Cor. 5:21). However, to enjoy that new relationship in daily fellowship (cf. days of Unleavened Bread which followed Passover), known sin must not be tolerated, but must be confessed and forsaken (cf. I John 1:5–10).

C. Keep the Feast (5:8)

1. The command stated

This command to "keep the feast" comes as the result of the other two commands ("therefore," *hōste*). Instead of using the typical direct imperative ("keep ye"), he included himself in the admonition: "Let us keep." Paul did not charge them to do something which he himself was not willing to follow. Although the feast does not specifically refer to the ordinance of the Lord's Table or to the communal meal eaten before that event, it does include them. Keeping the feast involves all areas of the Christian life, both within and without the normal functions of the local church.

2. The command explained

Three prepositional phrases (introduced by "with," *en*) show the sphere or manner in which the feast is to be kept. The first two are negative and the third is positive. The "old leaven" refers to both the sinning member and the church's toleration of his presence in their midst. "Malice" (*kakias*) emphasizes the principle of sin; "wickedness" (*ponērias*), its practice. One who acts with *kakias* does wrong; one who acts with *ponērias* does wrong with great pleasure (cf. Rom. 1:18, 32). Rather, sincerity and truth should mark Christian fellowship. "Sincerity" contains the purity of motive and "truth" the purity of action. They include both the heart and the mind and both moral and doctrinal excellence. The word for "sincerity" (*eilikriveias*) literally means "judged by the sun." It was used of any object through which the sun could shine without revealing any crack or flaw.

D. Separate from Fornicators (5:9–11)[12]

The principle is now clear. Believers are not "to get themselves mixed up with" (literal meaning of *synanamignusthai*) fornicators (cf. II Thess. 3:14). Paul states that he had written this to them in a previous epistle (5:9).

1. Unsaved fornicators (5:10)

Apparently the Corinthians misunderstood and misapplied the original command for separation. This produced confusion which Paul had to correct. Their inconsistency can be seen in their fellowship with a fornicator who was a professing Christian and their lack of contact with unsaved fornicators. This was exactly the opposite of that which Paul wanted them to do.

The opening words ("yet not altogether") mean "not in all circumstances." Paul fully expected that situations would rise in which believers must necessarily be involved with unsaved, immoral men. Athough Christians are not of the world, they are still in the world (John 17:14–15). They live next door to the unsaved; work with, over, and under the unsaved; and go to shopping malls and parks along with the unsaved. This contact cannot and should not be avoided. In fact, it should be welcomed as an opportunity to witness. Paul's logic is further expressed at the end of the verse: "[If absolutely no contact with the unsaved was what I meant], then must ye needs go out of the world." The only way to avoid such contact is for the Christian to die and go to heaven. Becoming a recluse is not the answer, either.

Paul used this occasion to enlarge on the principle which beforehand specifically applied only to the immoral. Note the three groups of men as indicated by the threefold use of "with."[13] The first, "fornicators," naturally referred to those who had sinned against their bodies, the sexually immoral people. The second group[14] represents those who have sinned against

---

[12]Consult the section, "Lost Letter," in the Introduction, pp. xv-xvii.

[13]The Greek text separates the groups by the use of the connective *ē*.

[14]The Granville Sharp rule is seen here. This is one group identified by two sins.

others. The "covetous" are possessed by the lust to have more money and property, usually that belonging to another (cf. 6:10; Eph. 5:5). They defraud for the sake of gain. The "extortioners" are those who steal or seize something from others (cf. Luke 18:11). In crime, they could be thieves or robbers of any type. In commerce, they can take what is not due them or take advantage of someone's financial plight. The third group, the "idolaters," are those who have sinned against the very nature of God (Rom. 1:21–23, 25). In the first century, almost the entire Roman world was devoted to idolatry. Pagan temples and idols were everywhere. There was no way for Christians to escape contact from that atmosphere.

2. Saved fornicators (5:11)

The situation is altogether different for a professing Christian who is involved in immorality or any other public sin. It really does not matter whether the person is a genuine believer or simply one who calls himself a Christian without being one.

Bas relief of Bacchus, god of wine.

Since he is "called a brother," the basis of contact between the church and that individual is the opposite of that between the church and a known, unsaved immoral person. The church corporately and individually, is "not to eat" with him. This refers to both the observance of the Lord's Table and the eating of ordinary meals in the home. A Christian can accept an invitation to dinner by an unsaved person (10:27), but he should refuse an invitation given by an unrepentant, professing Christian. Two can only walk [eat] together if they are agreed (cf. Amos 3:3). Although Christ ate with publicans and sinners, He did not acknowledge them as His followers nor did He condone their trespasses. If believers are to have any social contact with sinning, professing Christians, it must be done without any acknowledgment of the latter as brothers in Christ. Certainly believers are not to initiate and to tolerate fellowship with an immoral, professing Christian when the church has already taken official action to purge him from their assembly.

The restriction on fellowship was expanded to include others beside the known fornicator in their midst. The idolater was a Christian whose participation in the heathen diet and festivals actually manifested an acceptance of the pagan rites (8:7–10; 10:20-21; cf. I John 5:21). The railer is a person who speaks harshly of others by using abusive language (cf. Matt. 5:22). The phrase, "with such," demonstrates that the exclusion goes beyond the listed six categories to any notorious sin.

E. Put Away the Sinner (5:12–13)

To demonstrate further that the command to separate did not have for its object the unsaved, Paul disclaimed any right to judge the unbelievers ("them also that are without"). The unsaved were outside his jurisdiction. Their behavior was to be expected — after all, they were only living in accordance with their lost position before a holy God. However, Christians have both the right and the responsibility to judge unrepentant members within their local church.[15] Parents have the right to discipline their own children, but they have no authority to chastise their neighbor's children for the same faults. This does not

---

[15]The question implies an affirmative answer.

71

mean that the unsaved will go unpunished for their sins. Since all sin is ultimately against God, only God is judging and will judge men for their immoral behavior (Rom. 2:5; Heb. 13:4; I Peter 4:17; Rev. 20:11–15).[16]

Paul then ended this major section with a clear command: "Therefore put away from among yourselves that wicked person" (cf. Deut. 17:7; 24:7). This was their responsibility. The verb literally means: "Lift out of" or "Take up out of" (*exarate*). They were to take decisive action;[17] there was to be no delay in the administration of the charge. They were to be like surgeons, removing the cancer by operation, not by medication.

QUESTIONS FOR DISCUSSION

1. Are there any sins which are more frequently found in Christian circles than among the unsaved? If so, what are they, and why is this so?

2. Why are churches reluctant to discipline their members? What can be done to improve this situation?

3. Are you aware of any churches that have lost their effectiveness because of the toleration of unrepentant members?

4. Should the observance of the Lord's Table be supervised or policed by the pastor and the church officers? If so, to what extent?

5. Why do Christians often fail to grieve over others who have fallen into notorious sins?

6. Reconcile Paul's command to judge with Christ's charge not to judge (Matt. 7:1).

7. What involvements with the unsaved are good? What involvements with the unsaved are bad?

[16]The word "judgeth" is *krinei*. In the Greek, it can be either in the present or in the future tense. The only difference is in the position of the accent mark. This is somewhat subjective because accent marks were not part of the original writings.

[17]The verb is an aorist imperative. It is based upon the same verb translated "be taken away" (5:2).

5

Lawsuits and Sexual Purity
I Corinthians 6

In this chapter, Paul deals with two more problems that were reported to him by the household of Chloe and/or the three church messengers. The subjects of lawsuits between Christians and of sexual sin are not mutually exclusive, although it does seem strange to the casual reader that Paul inserted the litigation matter between the sections on sexual abuse (5:1–13; cf. 6:12–20; followed by the chapter on marriage). Fornication and covetousness, though, are grouped together in this context as similar sins (5:10–11; 6:9–10). Both stem from false, evil desires — one for financial satisfaction and the other for physical pleasure.

I. LAWSUITS (6:1–11)

The previous section ended with the theme of judging. Believers have the right, ability, and responsibility to judge their lawless members, but only God has the right to judge the unsaved (5:12–13). That truth serves as the transition to this new problem. If believers are not to judge the unsaved, why should believers let the unsaved judge them?

A. Their Problem (6:1)

The divisive spirit was so strong that one Christian dared to bring a lawsuit against his fellow believer. The audacity of that action can be seen in the abrupt question that the apostle used to introduce this problem.[1] The "matter" (*pragma*)[2] that produced the clash was not over spiritual issues, but rather over "things pertaining to this life" (*biōtika*, 6:3–4). This refers to money and property. Such disagreements are bound to come during this earthly existence. Paul recognized that, but he was radically opposed to their method of resolving the conflict.

They chose to "go to law"[3] before pagan judges. Although Paul exercised his Roman citizenship in using the civil legal system (Acts 16:37–39; 25:10–11), he used it as a last resort and never in a dispute with a professing Christian. He did not assert that the courts were corrupt, nor that the believers would be unable to receive a fair hearing. Rather, Christians should not parade any of their differences before the world. Family disputes should be settled within the family. It was inconsistent for those who had a justified standing before God to appear before "the unjust" (cf. "unbelievers," 6:6) in order to receive justice.

B. Their Ignorance (6:2–6)

Although the church boasted about its wisdom, in this chapter Paul chastises it six times for its ignorance (6:2, 3, 9, 15, 16, 19). All six criticisms are contained within rhetorical questions that suggest an affirmative answer.[4]

1. Saints will judge the world (6:2)

Daniel predicted that the saints would judge when the kingdom would be established by the Messiah (Dan. 7:22). Christ informed the apostles that they would rule over the twelve tribes of Israel (Matt. 19:28). Paul knew that reigning followed suffering (II Tim. 2:12). One of the blessings of the first resurrection is to share in Christ's millennial rule (Rev. 2:26–27; 3:23; 20:4). In that day, resurrected believers will judge and rule over a planet

---

[1]The word "dare" is very emphatic, standing first in the Greek text.

[2]This word was used in the papyri for formal lawsuits.

[3]The verb *krinesthai* is a permissive middle voice infinitive. They permitted themselves to be judged in this manner.

[4]The use of the negative *ouk* with the verb for innate or implied knowledge (*oidate*) falls within this grammatical rule.

inhabited both by believers in natural bodies who came into the kingdom out of the tribulation and by unsaved persons who are born after the kingdom has started.

The argument is obvious. If believers in that future day are to have such an important task of judging, why do they view themselves as incompetent to make decisions about petty issues? This word for "matters" (*kritērion*) is different than that in verse 1 (*pragma*). It refers to the least important courts or the smallest tribunals. Their future responsibility ("judge the world") was like the Supreme Court in comparison to a justice of the peace ("judge the smallest matters").

2. Saints will judge angels (6:3)

Spiritual Christians today are a cause for laughter by both evil angels and the world (4:9), but in the future both will be judged by the believer. Some evil angels are already chained in darkness awaiting the time of judgment (II Peter 2:4; Jude 6). It is clear that holy angels will assist God in the overthrow of Satan and his evil angels (Gen. 3:15; Rev. 12:7–9; 20:1–3), but this is the only passage that teaches that believers will also share in the judgment of wicked angels. The fact is certain, but the time is not revealed. Perhaps it will occur at the beginning of the millennial kingdom and/or at the Great White Throne Judgment (Rev. 20:4–6; cf. 20:11–15).

Again, the application is plain. If believers are to judge the world of supernatural beings, should they not be able to cope with natural decisions about the ordinary things of life? The emphatic phrase "how much more" (translation of one word, *mētige*) reinforces that conclusion.

3. Saints should judge themselves (6:4–6)

Whenever the problem arose again,[5] Paul wanted the church to establish those who were least esteemed by the world as the judges over these differences (cf. 1:28 — same word). Spiritual believers, even though they are not qualified legally, still make

---

[5]This is indicated by the protasis ("if" clause) using *ean* with the subjunctive verb. Note also that Paul combined the "judgments" (6:3) into this one problem area.

The Bema tribunal, among the ruins of ancient Corinth.

better judges over brotherly disputes than unbelievers who have legal credentials.[6]

Their willingness to have the pagan courts arbitrate was a shameful deed (6:5a). This situation was entirely different from the problem of pride and church divisions (cf. 4:14). In that case, as a concerned spiritual father, he did not want to shame them for their supposed spiritual superiority. However, he now saw the feeling of shame as a proper motivation, especially since they had felt constrained to go to the world for a decision.

In his question,[7] Paul again used sarcastic irony (6:5b). They prided themselves on their wisdom, and yet, in their willingness to go to the pagan courts, they were admitting publicly that there was no one in their church capable of rendering a fair judgment. Actually, they *did* have such wise discerners within their

[6]The apodosis (conclusion clause) has been viewed as a question, a statement of fact, and as an imperative. Based upon the conditional clause, the third option seems to be the most likely.

[7]The Authorized Version has two questions, but the Greek construction favors the joining of the two into one.

number.[8] The infinitive "to judge" means to give a decision, not to conduct a trial.[9]

Unfortunately, Paul received the report and wrote the epistle after the legal action had already been taken (6:6).[10] It was bad enough for believers to have disputes with each other over temporal, material matters, but the situation was made worse when they decided to go to law. However, what made that even worse (indicated by "and that") was their appearance before the unsaved judges. The apostle had wished that they would have settled for arbitration (*diakrinai*, 6:5) from the Christians within the church rather than judgment (*krinesthai*, 6:1) by the pagans outside the church.

C. Their Solution (6:7–11)

If nothing could have been gained, Paul would never have written this section. What was done was done. However, there were valuable lessons that the Corinthian Christians needed to learn from this experience in order that they might not repeat these sins.

1. Admit their sin (6:7–8)

Confession precedes progression. Both the church and the actual participants in the litigation had to admit their error in the handling of the problem before the church could go forward. The church sinned in tolerating the action of its members and in failing to provide leadership. Naturally, the participants sinned in their hostile attitude toward each other and in their presence before the pagan judicial system. The word "fault" (*hēttēma*) means "a worsening, a defeat." To take the issue before unbelievers was to incur a defeat no matter what the decision turned out to be. There would be no winners, only losers.

In a series of two questions, Paul pointed out that they should have passively accepted ill treatment rather than demand-

[8]The question uses a double negative construction and implies an affirmative answer.

[9]It is in the aorist tense rather than the present.

[10]This is indicated by the strong adversative "but" (*alla*) and by the present indicative verb.

ing their rights (6.7b).[11] Christ taught nonresistance (Matt. 5:39). He also instructed, "And if any man will sue thee at the law, and take away thy coat, let him have thy cloak also" (Matt. 5:40). Believers are not to render evil for evil or to seek vengeance (Rom. 12:17, 19). Elsewhere Paul wrote, ". . . if any man have a quarrel against any: even as Christ forgave you, so also do ye. And above all these things put on [love], which is the bond of perfectness" (Col. 3:13–14). When Christ was on the cross, "he threatened not; but committed himself to him that judgeth righteously" (I Peter 2:23). Believers should always do likewise.

Not only were the Corinthian Christians wrong in refusing to accept injustice committed against them; they also sinned in defrauding others (6:8).[12] They were rendering evil for evil rather than overcoming evil with good (Rom. 12:17, 21). They were not only recipients of ill treatment, but they were also initiating it. The final phrase ("and that your brethren") shows how far they had veered from Christ's plain commands. Morris aptly observed: "The Corinthians were committing a double sin. They were sinning against ethical standards, and they were sinning against brotherly love."[13]

2. Recognize the position of the unsaved (6:9–10)

In this passage, Paul affirmed twice that the unsaved would "not inherit the kingdom of God." This judgment is based both on the unbeliever's position (6:9a) and practice (6:10b). The inference is evident. Why should Christians, who are heirs of God and joint heirs with Christ (Rom. 8:17; Gal. 4:7), submit themselves to those whose character and conduct will prevent them from entering into the kingdom? The term "unrighteous" is the same word translated "unjust" (6:1). It refers to the unjustified standing of the lost, although it also could include their sinful behavior.

Regardless of his religious profession (cf. 5:11), a person whose life-style is habitually marked by any of these catalogued sins is not saved (cf. I John 3:6–10). A Christian is "deceived" if

[11]Both verbs are in the passive voice. Also note the double use of "rather."

[12]The two verbs in this verse are changed to the active voice.

[13]Leon Morris, *The First Epistle of Paul to the Corinthians*, p. 95.

he thinks that there is no correlation between spiritual position and practice (James 2:14, 18). Since the term "idolaters" falls within the groups dealing with physical immorality, it apparently points out those who had sexual relations with temple priests and priestesses. The "effeminate" (based upon a word meaning "soft") refers to homosexuals, whereas the "abusers of themselves with mankind" could refer to sadistic, sexual perverts. Thieves are those who steal secretly, rather than by force.

3. Rejoice in their salvation (6:11)

A sharp contrast is drawn between their past practice and their present position (seen in the threefold use of the strong adversative "but," alla). They were to recognize that God had saved them from the very life-styles of those before whom they were taking their petty differences. The opening phrase ("and such were some of you") indicates that God not only can save all types of sinners, but that He had already done so for several members of their own church. Salvation involves not only a past deliverance from the guilt and penalty of sin, but also a daily release from the power and practice of sin (Titus 2:11–14). Their lives were now radically different.

The meanings of the three verbs — "washed," "sanctified," and "justified" which depict the believers' unalterable standing, indicate that these acts of God occur at the very moment of salvation. Hodge observes, "Their sins, considered as filth, had been washed away; considered as pollution, they had been purged or purified; considered as guilt, they had been covered with the righteousness of God."[14] The verb "washed" refers to the cleansing of regeneration (Ezek. 36:25; John 3:5; Titus 3:5). This nonrepeatable event removes the moral guilt from the believing sinner and gives him a permanent position of spiritual cleanliness (cf. John 13:10).[15] Some have identified this washing with

---

[14]Charles Hodge, Commentary on the First Epistle to the Corinthians, p. 99. The three verbs are aorist passive indicative.

[15]The eleven apostles did not have to repeat the spiritual bath of regeneration in order to have fellowship with Christ. They needed to have daily cleansing through confession of specific sins. The aorist middle verb could be translated: "You submitted yourselves to be washed." This emphasizes the exercise of will in saving faith.

water baptism. If that had been Paul's intent, he could have used the Greek word for baptism. Also, the order would be wrong if that had been the case. Water baptism follows, not precedes, justification. The word "sanctified" refers to positional sanctification (cf. 1:20), the act of God whereby the believing sinner is forever set apart from the world unto God. The verb "justified" refers to that act of God whereby He declares righteous that sinner who has been made righteous through faith in Christ.

The sphere of this threefold work of God can be seen in the two prepositional phrases (both introduced by *en* translated as "in" and "by"). The "name" of Jesus Christ stands for all that He is and all that He has done in His redemptive death and resurrection. This provides the authoritative basis for their salvation. The Spirit is the divine agent through whom the divine program of redemption is applied to the life of the believing sinner.

II. SEXUAL PURITY (6:12–20)

This is a strategic, transitional passage within the book. The subject of fornication had already been introduced and discussed somewhat (5:1, 9–11; 6:9). The first topic to be treated in the section dealing with questions raised in their letter concerns fornication and the sexual relations of husbands and wives (7:1–5). Thus, basic teaching on the Christian's body and sexual desires was needed, especially since many of the Gentile believers brought into their new experience pagan concepts about the body.

A. Principles For the Body (6:12–13a)

Four principles are given so that the believer might fulfill the desires of his body according to divine standards.

1. All things are lawful

This, of course, does not include those activities expressly forbidden in Scripture (6:9–10; cf. Exod. 20:1–17). Sin is always wrong and lawless, not lawful (I John 3:4). Paul meant that the satisfaction of divinely given physical desires ("all things") was within the will of God for every believer. God implanted within the bodies of men and women certain functions and drives which in themselves are proper and good. Included among these are the craving for food, the need of drink, and sexual attraction.

2. *All things are not expedient*

Note Paul's emphatic use of the pivotal "but." These desires have limitations under which they may be fulfilled. Their satisfaction cannot take place at any time, in any place, and under all circumstances. Gluttony, drunkenness, and premarital and extramarital sexual relations are all violations of these desires.

3. *Slavery is to be avoided*

The third principle again balances the first. ". . . I will not be brought under the power of any." The satisfaction of these desires must not become a god, a life-compelling force to obey whenever the desire beckons. Otherwise, man has reduced himself to the level of the animal creation rather than manifesting his exalted position as God's image-bearer.

4. *Desires are only temporary*

God created food so that it would satisfy the needs of the physical stomach. He also designed the stomach so that it could use the food for its satisfaction and health. However, the purposes of both food and the natural stomach will be rendered inoperative[16] at death and in the subsequent resurrection body. There will be no sexual relations in eternity (Matt. 22:30), and although the resurrection body will have the ability to eat (Luke 24:41–43), there is no indication that it will need to eat. It is "the belly," and not "the body," that "God shall destroy."

B. Purposes of the Body (6:13b–14)

Paul anticipated the logical rationalizations of the immoral. Since natural desires (food, drink, sex) are temporary, their use and/or misuse will not affect the soul nor the resurrection body. Paul, however, made a distinction between the natural body and the organs within that body ("body" vs. "belly"). The body is not to be identified with any one organ, nor is it simply the sum total of all of its organs.

---

[16]The verb *katargēsei*, translated as "destroy," does not mean annihilation, but rather the cessation of functions.

Thus, God never designed the body (total person with spiritual, mental, emotional, and physical needs) to be used for sinful, selfish gratification (6:13b). Rather, He structured the body to meet the needs and purposes of God Himself ("but for the Lord"); also, the body was so made that God could meet the needs of the body ("and the Lord for the body"). If the body is not used for the honor and glory of God (10:31), then the body has been misused. Although bodily functions cease at death, the purpose of the body continues. This can be seen in the doctrinal truth of the resurrection (6:14). Since the Father raised up Christ, He will also raise up each believer. The body, therefore, is very crucial to God's program of redemption. In fact, spiritual identification with Christ involves physical identification as well (6:15a; cf. Eph. 5:30). The believer cannot separate his body from his soul as he seeks to grow spiritually. It involves the commitment of his total being.

C. Perversion of the Body (6:15–18)

1. Believers should recognize their union with Christ (6:15)

Paul was shocked by their ignorance over sexual matters (6:15, 16, 19). Using questions and basic logic, he showed them why it was spiritually inconsistent for them to be involved in any form of sexual perversion. Since their bodies were "the members of Christ" (12:12), to commit fornication would be the same as making the members of Christ the members of a prostitute. How unthinkable! "God forbid!" Would Christ ever lie with a harlot? Never! And yet, because of their spiritual union with Christ, they were involving Him physically in fornication. They were taking away their bodies from proper use within the body of Christ for improper use in selfish gratification.

2. Believers should avoid union with harlots (6:16–17)

Not only is fornication contrary to the believer's union with Christ (6:15), it directly involves a physical union with the harlot (6:16). The act of sexual intercourse physically makes the two parties "one flesh." This union was designed by God as the climax of marital oneness, reflecting the spiritual, mental, and emotional unity already expressed and given (cf. Gen. 2:24). The verb "is joined" was used of gluing two pieces into one. No one could argue that he was simply being joined physically, and not mentally or emotionally. The sexual act involves a total, not a partial, oneness. This is why the sin was so odious when committed by a believer.

Spiritual union should govern physical union (6:17). Marriage to Christ ("one spirit") should forbid union with a prostitute ("one body"; probably a pagan temple priestess). If a believer dishonors his vows to Christ, then he has committed not only physical fornication, but also spiritual adultery and/or bigamy.

3. Believers should flee sexual sin (6:18)

There is only one preventive solution: "Flee fornication." This is basic and simple, but it is also very true. Note that Paul uses the present tense. The intent of the command is, "Keep on fleeing" or "Make it your habit to flee." Joseph did (Gen. 39:10, 12), but David did not (II Sam. 11:2–4). Elsewhere Paul admonished, "But put ye on the Lord Jesus Christ, and make not provision for the flesh, to fulfill the lusts thereof" (Rom. 13:14).

The reason for abstinence from sexual sin is its effect within the body. The word "sin" emphasizes its result rather than its act (*hamartēma* rather than *hamartia*). A contrast is established between "without the body" (*ektos tou sōmatos*) and "against his own body" (*eis to idion sōma*).[17] Morris wrote: "Other sins against the body, e.g., drunkenness or gluttony, involve the use of that which comes from without the body. The sexual appetite rises from within."[18] The natural desires of the body become sinful when done in excess, but the sexual act is sinful in itself when done within fornication.

D. Possession of the Body (6:19–20)

Paul's clinching argument for sexual purity is the ownership of the believer's body. To whom does it really belong: self or God?

---

[17]Some commentators have suggested that the phrase, "Every sin that a man doeth is without the body," was a much quoted slogan of the Corinthians. It meant that all physical sins could not harm the real self.

[18]Morris, *Corinthians*, p. 102.

1. Believers are indwelt by God (6:19)

He first pointed out that the physical body of the Christian is "the temple of the Holy Spirit." The word for "temple" (*naos*) was used for the inner sanctuary, the most holy place where God dwelt, not for the general temple area.[19] The temple also belonged to God (cf. Matt. 21:13). Christ's body was also a temple (John 2:19). He not only belonged to God; He was God, and later filled the earthly temple with the glory of His presence. Because of the indwelling ministry of the Spirit, the believer's body is sacred, designed for godly purposes, and owned by God.

Both the indwelling ("in you") and the possession ("which ye have") of the Spirit are given by God ("of God"). The believer did not work for salvation or the indwelling presence of the Spirit; both are eternal gifts from God.

The believer therefore does not belong to himself. His very personality (intellect, emotions, and will), his ambitions and abilities, and his body with all of its desires are not his to command and to please. He totally belongs to His divine occupant.

2. Believers are bought by God (6:20)

The final reason of divine ownership is the fact that all believers were redeemed from the penalty and power of sin with the price of Christ's precious death (I Peter 1:18–19; II Peter 2:1). Christ bought each Christian. The right of ownership goes with the price of redemption. The verb "redeemed" (*ēgorasthēte*) points to the provision at the cross and to the appropriation at the time of conversion. It is a summary term, including the previously mentioned spiritual blessings (6:11). Believers never did own themselves. Once they were owned by sin, but they were purchased from that slavery to be owned by the divine master.

Since the believer belongs to God, there is only one purpose that should mark his will: Glorify God. In his body with its natural desires and in his spirit,[20] he should magnify his new

[19]Indirectly, this serves as a proof for the deity of the Holy Spirit. Note the logic: The temple was where God dwelt; the Holy Spirit indwelt the temple; therefore the Holy Spirit must be God.

[20]The critical Greek text omits the words "and in your spirit, which are God's." It is true that the emphasis of this section is on the body; but the glorification of God involves the total being of man, not just one part.

owner (his Creator, Savior, and Lord), rather than gratify his selfish lusts.

QUESTIONS FOR DISCUSSION

1. Is there any justification for a Christian to take another believer into court? What about swindle, default on installment payments, or disagreement over property lines?

2. Should the Biblical principles for handling material disputes between Christians be written into the church constitution?

3. Should the principle of taking wrong ever be nullified on account of the large amount of financial fraud — hundreds or thousands of dollars?

4. In a church split, how should property rights be determined?

5. How can the church have a greater ministry to those unsaved who are marked by Paul's list of sins (6:9–10)?

6. In spite of Biblical directives, what sometimes causes a Christian to get involved in fornication? What can be done to prevent it from happening? Would more serious Bible study be helpful? How about sermons or literature?

7. What effects do different sins have on the body? Are they permanent or temporary?

The Principles Governing Marriage
I Corinthians 7

With this chapter, Paul begins to deal with the topical questions submitted in a letter sent to the apostle ("Now concerning the things whereof ye wrote unto me . . ."). Although this letter has been lost, its contents can be known through the answers given by Paul. These matters included marital problems (7:1–24), virgins (7:25), food offered to idols (8:1), responsibilities of women within the church (11:2), the communion service (11:17), spiritual gifts (12:1), the doctrine of physical resurrection (15:1), and a special relief collection (16:1).[1]

Although the order of the letter of inquiry is unknown, Paul chose to answer their questions about marital problems first, probably because he had just discussed the sexual desires of the believer's body (6:12–20). This common content forms a natural link between the two major sections of the book.

I. SEXUAL INTIMACIES (7:1–7)

Contrary to popular opinion, the Bible is not against sex. God created men and women with sexual desires. In themselves, the desires are not morally wrong. What makes them sinful are lustful motivations, abuses, and misuses outside of the divine purpose.

A. For Singles (7:1)

The principle is clear. Premarital sexual relationships are

---

[1]Some of the topics are clearly marked by the phrase "now concerning" (*peri de;* 7:1, 25; 8:1; 12:1; 16:1). The others are self-evident from the change of content.

forbidden for single people. Elsewhere Paul wrote, "For this is the will of God, even your sanctification, that ye should abstain from fornication" (I Thess. 4:3). The infinitive "to touch" refers to the stimulation of the physical organs with resulting sexual embrace. This counsel is simply an extension of the seventh commandment: "Thou shalt not commit adultery" (Exod. 20:14).

However, some believe that this verse teaches that the single, celibate life is commendable.[2] Paul did not say that it was necessary or better to remain single; rather, that it was "good" (*kalon*)[3] to do so. This is not a moral good *(agathon)* since the apostle later approved the marital union (7:28, 36). Future heresies were against marriage (I Tim. 4:3), but this is contrary to the creative purposes for man and woman (Gen. 2:18; Heb. 13:4). Paul's counsel was doubtless based upon the living conditions in Corinth, which were not conducive to a normal marriage relationship (7:26, 29, 32, 35). It also served as a reproof for those who argued that marriage was necessary for all in order to live a fulfilled life.

B. For Couples (7:2–5)

1. Marriage is usually necessary (7:2)

Marriage, however, was commanded[4] to avoid the sins of premarital and extramarital fornication. The opening phrase literally reads, "on account of the fornications" (note the plural). The believers at Corinth were surrounded by sinful temptations and excesses that constantly warred against the spiritual control of their sexual desires. In such a situation, a wholesome marital union was not only helpful, but absolutely necessary for many. The command (7:2) shows that the fulfillment of sexual needs within the marriage relationship is right, that only monogamy should be practiced, that sexual fidelity is enjoined upon each

[2]Leon Morris, *The First Epistle of Paul to the Corinthians*, p. 105. Also A. T. Robertson, *Word Pictures in the New Testament*, 4:124.

[3]Paul again used this concept in later verses (7:8, 26).

[4]The English word "let" seems to imply permission, but it is only a helping verb used to translate the third person Greek imperative.

partner, and that celibacy is not the norm for the majority of believers.

2. Marital partners should meet the sexual needs of each other (7:3)

The husband is to take the initiative in this area (his command is given first). Marriage without sex is not only unnatural, but it is expressly forbidden. The word "benevolence" (*opheilēn*) refers to the conjugal or sexual rights. The command ("render") indicates that sexual intimacies should be a constant part of the marital union, not limited to the honeymoon or to the purposes of bearing children (cf. Prov. 5:18–19; Eccles. 9:9).

3. Marital partners belong to each other (7:4)

The bodies, including the sexual organs, of the husband and the wife belong to each other. This shows that the wife is not a piece of property to be used or exploited at will. She is not a sex object, existing only to satisfy her husband's whims. Rather, they are both persons who lovingly are to give themselves to each other. They are not to give or to withhold sexual privileges as the basis of reward or punishment. Each should be motivated not to have his own desires satisfied, but rather to fulfill the needs of the other.

4. Marital partners may temporarily abstain from sexual relationships (7:5)

Sexual abstinence must not be done unilaterally, but rather out of mutual consent. It must be done only temporarily and for a set time. The fulfillment of specific spiritual purposes ("fasting and prayer")[5] could require the abstinence of physical fulfillment. The word "school" comes from the verb "give" (*scholasēte*). Both parties, in order to learn maximum spiritual truth, could agree to forego sexual privileges in order to devote their total energies to higher priorities. However, they should resume sexual intimacies before they are tempted by Satan to fulfill their desires outside of the marital union. Christian couples who are sexually happy will not succumb to outside flirtations.

[5]The concept of fasting is not included in the Greek critical text.

C. Permitted or Commanded (7:6–7)

Paul was quick to point out that both the single life and the marital union are permitted, and not commanded. The duties for each commitment are prescribed, but neither institution is obligatory. Marriage is a *may,* not a *must.* Nowhere does the Bible state, "Thou shalt marry," or "Thou shalt not marry."

Perrin wrongly observed: "The full humanity of the apostle is evident in this passage as we see him striving to give advice in matters on which he was by no means an expert."[6] This approach views the Bible only as a mere human composition, not as God's revealed word through Spirit-directed men. This verse actually shows that Paul knew the difference between inspired advice and divinely imparted directives.

Because Paul was single and had no compelling urge to be married and to have sexual relationships, he was able to devote his entire life to the Christian ministry (7:7). This brought him spiritual fulfillment, and he desired this goal for every believer. However, he recognized that both the single life and the marital union were gifts from God (*charisma*). Men and women must act according to that desire divinely implanted within them, not in opposition to it. Christ also explained that concept (Matt. 19:10–12).

II. UNMARRIED AND WIDOWS (7:8–9)

The words "I say therefore" introduce a slight change in subject. Paul now applied the previous general principles to two specific groups, "the unmarried" (*tois agamois*) and "the widows" (*tais chērais*). Since the latter term refers to women who had lost their husbands through death, the former probably includes men who had lost their wives through death. Possibly the term might include both widowers and men who had never been married, but it certainly would not include divorced men.[7]

Again, Paul viewed it as personally "good" (*kalon*) not necessarily morally "good" (*agathon*) if the two groups chose to remain unmarried. However, he knew that, since they had formerly

[6]Norman Perrin, *The New Testament: An Introduction,* p. 103.

[7]However, the singular *agamos* is used of a wife who has departed from her husband (7:11).

received the gift of marriage, they might not be able to control the desires for sex and companionship within them ("if they cannot contain"). In their case, it was "better" (again, "not commanded") to marry than to try to live socially with unfulfilled desires which could lead to emotional distress and spiritual defeat ("to burn").

III. CHRISTIAN COUPLES (7:10–11)

Since mixed couples are mentioned in the next set of verses (7:12–16), the class Paul refers to as "the married" must refer to Christian couples. Paul's commands to them are exactly what Christ Himself taught (Matt. 5:32; 19:3–9; Mark 10:2–12; Luke 16:18).

Four directives are given. First, the wife should not "depart from" or be separated from her husband.[8] The papyri contain references where this verb ("depart") is a technical term for divorce. Second, if the departure has already taken place or if it occurs in spite of the directive, the wife is to "remain unmarried." No cause for the departure is given here. There is no implication for a remarriage to a different partner in case of adultery or willful desertion.[9] Third, the wife should attempt to "be reconciled to her husband." Fourth, the husband should not initiate separation or divorce by "putting away" or leaving (aphienai, the same word used for remission of sins in I John 1:9) his wife. The first three commands focus on the wife, whereas the fourth centers on the husband. The term "married" actually implies that marriage is a permanent relationship.[10]

[8]The verb "depart" is an aorist passive imperative (chōristhēnai). It implies that the departure was forced upon her.

[9]Boyer thus argues that all divorce was forbidden by Christ. James Boyer, For a World Like Ours, p. 979. However, Harry Ironside (I Corinthians, p. 207), Charles Hodge (Commentary on the First Epistle to the Corinthians, p. 113), and A. T. Robertson (Word Pictures, 4:107) see adultery as a basis for divorce and remarriage.

[10]It is a perfect active participle (gegamēkosin). The act of marriage introduces a permanent union.

IV. MIXED COUPLES (7:12–16)

A. The Marriage Should Continue (7:12–13)

Since Christians should not marry unbelievers (7:39; II Cor. 6:14), this problem of mixed marriage resulted when one of the partners became saved after marriage. Does God sanction the marital bonds of two unsaved people? Does the salvation of one partner annul the union? The answer is clear. The Christian husband should not divorce nor leave the unsaved wife if she desires to maintain the marriage under the new circumstances (7:12). Also, the Christian wife should not divorce nor "leave" ("put away" and "leave" are the same word in the Greek; *aphietō*; cf. 7:11) the unsaved husband if he desires to maintain the marital union (7:13). After the captivity, Jews were permitted to put away their Gentile wives (Ezra 9:1 — 10:44), but that historical precedent has no application to the marriage between a Christian and an unbeliever.

B. Reasons for Continuing the Marriage (7:14)

1. The sanctification of the unsaved partner

The explanatory connective "for" introduces the reasons for continuing the marriage. In the spiritual realm, uncleanness adversely affects that which is clean, and not vice versa (Hag. 2:11–13). However, the unsaved partner does receive spiritual benefits or advantages now that his partner has become a Christian. The unsaved husband or wife has become "sanctified" (*hēgiastai*) in the salvation of the other partner. This does not mean that the person is saved, because his salvation is still viewed as a future possibility (7:16). Rather, since God in His sovereignty has saved one partner in a marriage, the unsaved partner has now been set apart for a special work of conviction by the Holy Spirit through the testimony and the changed behavior of the Christian partner.

2. The sanctification of the children

The same principle applies to the children. The departure of the believing partner from the home would leave the children totally unaffected by the cleansing effects of that person's salvation. The presence and ministry of the saved partner within the home guarantees that the children have also been set apart by the Holy Spirit. The salvation of the unsaved partner and children is more likely if the one member of the family who has become saved remains in the home.

C. Reason for Ending the Marriage (7:15–16)

The believing partner is under no obligation to maintain the marital union if the unsaved member initiates the separation or divorce. Grosheide astutely observed, "If the believing party were under obligation to prevent the departure he would be subject to the unbeliever and would virtually be forced to abandon his or her faith since only by doing that could a divorce be prevented."[11] What follows the removal of "bondage"? There is room for disagreement here. Some believe that the deserted Christian partner is now free to remarry,[12] but others feel that remarriage is not introduced into the problem and that the saved partner has only been released from all attempts to keep the marriage together.[13]

The believing partner should recognize that God has called him or her to a position and practice of peace, not to conflict and hostility (7:15c). Through faith, he has a standing of peace (Rom. 5:1); through prayer, he has a daily, protecting peace (Phil. 4:6–7); and through the Spirit, he has the fruit of peace (Gal. 5:22). Peace should mark the marital relationship, whether it involves the maintenance of the union or the acceptance of the willful separation desired by the unsaved member.

The believing partner should recognize that God can use the union or the separation as a means to "save" the unbelieving member (7:16). However, the marriage should not be maintained solely as a basis for evangelism. To hold desperately to the marriage even though the unsaved partner wants to end it is not wise. Paul's question, therefore, can be viewed from two different perspectives.

[11]F. W. Grosheide, *Commentary on the First Epistle to the Corinthians*, p. 166.

[12]Ironside, *I Corinthians*, p. 213; Morris, *Corinthians*, p. 111; and Robertson, *Word Pictures*, p. 128.

[13]Boyer, *World Like Ours*, pp. 80–81. This is the position of the author.

V. PERMANENCE OF RELATIONSHIPS (7:17–24)

In this section, Paul used racial and social illustrations to demonstrate the permanence of marital relationships.

A. Abide in Your Calling (7:17–20)

Paul first laid down a general principle: Christians should "walk" for the Lord (cf. Eph. 4:1) in the midst of that position or vocation in which God saved them (7:17). The "distribution" probably refers to the gifts of celibacy or marriage given to each person (7:7). The call of God to salvation (1:26) involves the time, the place, and the circumstances in which the person was regenerated. Paul also wanted the church to know that the directives which he gave to them were the same as he preached in all the other churches (7:17b).

Specifically, at salvation God did not make a Gentile out of a Jew; therefore a saved Jew should not attempt to become a non-Jew nor should he repudiate his Jewish heritage (17:18a). Also, an uncircumcised Gentile should not submit to the Jewish rite of circumcision after he has become a Christian (17:18b). It is obedience, not race, that brings the blessing of God (17:19). Paul earlier wrote, "For in Jesus Christ neither circumcision availeth anything, nor uncircumcision; but faith which worketh by love" (Gal. 5:6). Race or religious rites did not determine the call of God or improve one's acceptable standing in Christ (cf. Gal. 6:15).

A saved Jew and a saved Gentile are equally saved. God saved them when they were in their respective stations of life. He did it neither because of them nor in spite of them. Thus, they should "abide" (remain) in their racial calling.

B. Have No Anxiety in Your Calling (7:21–24)

From race, Paul moved to the social strata of slaves and free men. Since more than half of the Roman Empire was composed of slaves, many of the early Christians came out of the slave class. In the secular world, slavery was viewed as a badge of personal inferiority. To some converted slaves, this fact caused grave concern. Paul commanded them not to let their slave status be a cause of anxiety (cf. Phil. 4:6) lest they become spiritually ineffective. Rather, they should use their slavery as a means to glorify God (Eph. 6:5–8; Col. 3:22–25; I Peter 2:18–25).If they were able to become free (through the desire of the master or the payment of a ransom), they were also to use their social liberty as a means of honoring God.

Paradoxically, in Christ men are spiritually the opposite of what they are in the world (7:22). A natural slave in the world has been set free from the bondage of sin and is now the freeman of Christ. He should not let his temporal, human bondage rob him of the joy of his eternal, spiritual freedom (cf. John 8:36). Contrariwise, the freeman in the world, at conversion, becomes a spiritual slave. He must learn the principles of total submission to the will of his heavenly master (cf. Eph. 6:9; Col. 4:1). Both the natural slave and the freeman were slaves to sin and both were redeemed from their spiritual plight by the precious price of Christ's shed blood (7:23a; cf. I Peter 1:18–19). Since they were both bought, they both belong to Christ and owe their total allegiance to Him (6:19–20). A freeman voluntarily should not sell himself into human slavery, and the natural slave should see himself first as the possession of God. Divine obligations supercede human demands.

Paul then concluded with a repetition of his basic premise. Men should "abide" or remain content in that station of life in which God saved them. They should do so with the full assurance that God is with them in their circumstances and that they should live near God no matter what problems confront them (note the addition of the words "with God," 7:24).

VI. VIRGINS (7:25–35)

This new section is formally introduced by the phrase, "Now concerning virgins" (*peri de tōn parthenōn*). Although the word can be used of males (Rev. 14:4), it here refers primarily to females.[14] Concerning them, Christ did not speak when He was on earth nor did He reveal to Paul any commandments. However, the apostle chose to give his "judgment" (*gnōmēn* is related to the word for "knowledge," *gnōsis*), namely counsel based upon experience and observation. He cited two qualifications for his right to give this advice. First, he had obtained mercy and second, he was regarded as faithful by Christ. Both concepts in-

---

[14]However, men are definitely in the context (7:26, 27, 28a).

volve his salvation experience and his call into the apostolic ministry (cf. 4:2; II Cor. 4:1; I Tim 1:12). If anyone had a right to speak to this subject, it was Paul. Under the circumstances, it was the best counsel that anyone could give or receive.

A. Remain Single (7:26–28)

Paul used the word "good" twice to state again that the single life was to be preferred in the midst of their unique circumstances (7:26). No one knows for sure what the "present distress" was. Later, the apostle talked about "trouble in the flesh" (7:28) and the "shortness of time" (7:29). Perrin thinks it involves Paul's mistaken notion about the "imminent end of the world."[15] It probably refers to a specific economic, political, and religious crisis in Corinth, especially since Paul elsewhere commended marriage (Eph. 5:22 — 6:4; Col. 3:18–21; I Tim. 3:2; 5:14; Titus 1:6; 2:3–5). At that time, virginity was the best calling in which one could find himself.

In a series of two questions and two imperative answers (7:27), he pointed out that the single life should not be gained through attempts to be separated or divorced from one's marriage partner. However, if the marital union had been dissolved through death or possibly the willful desertion of the unbelieving partner, the "loosed" member would be better off if he did not attempt remarriage.

Since this section contains counsel and not commandment, Paul granted that marriage for a male virgin or a widower did not involve moral sin (7:28a). He then added that marriage for a female virgin was not a sin either, even under these desperate circumstances (7:28b). He gave a cautionary warning, however, that such marriages would bring instant problems into their lives and that he wanted them to be spared from these difficulties (7:28c).

B. Be Alert to the Brevity of Life (7:29–31)

The statement about the shortness of time cannot refer to Paul's belief in the imminent return of Christ, especially since the apostle made long-range plans himself (Rom. 15:24–25). It

[15]Perrin, N. T. Introduction.

must refer to the atmosphere of persecution at Corinth (cf. Acts 18:9, 12, 17) which made normal marital relationships difficult if not impossible. The loss of job through pagan pressure and/or the loss of life through martyrdom created an abnormal incubator for proper home life.

In a series of five comparisons (note the fivefold usage of "as"), Paul pointed out that believers should not be preoccupied with earthly circumstances. They should not permit the life of this world to determine and control their spiritual development (Heb. 11:13–16, 24–26). They were not to surrender their wives, weeping, rejoicing, buying, or use of this world. They are right and proper in their place, but there come times when they have to be balanced. Mourners can easily become engrossed in their sorrow (e.g., death of a loved one), rejoicers can be taken up with their happiness (e.g., marriage and honeymoon), buyers can concentrate on their new possessions (e.g., new car or home), and the users of the world can become enamored with it (Rom. 12:1–2; I John 2:15). Grosheide states that "marriage is something of this time, not of the proper abiding life of the Christian."[16] That observation is true of all of these experiences. Eternal duties and concepts should possess the believer rather than the temporal activities that mark this passing world.

C. Be Free of Care (7:32–35)

Paul's major concern was that the Corinthian Christians would not undertake new responsibilities that would increase their anxiety in this life (7:32a). The cares of this world, even though they are wholesome, can choke the fruitfulness of God's Word in one's life and keep him from experiencing total righteousness (Matt. 6:25; Mark 4:19). Marriage, in awkward situations, can do just that.

1. The care of the man (7:32–34)

If a man is unmarried, he can give undivided attention to Christian living and service. This would involve his time, abilities, energy, and money. In a sense, he could be like a consecrated Nazarite (Num. 6:1–8) like John the Baptist (Luke

---

[16]*Grosheide, Corinthians,* p. 177.

1:13–17). In His celibacy, Christ could say, ". . . I do always those things that please him [the Father]" (John 8:29). On the other hand, the married man must be concerned about food, clothing, and shelter in order to meet the needs of his wife and family. This is honorable; there is nothing wrong with it (I Tim. 5:8). Paul is simply stating facts, and he wants the Corinthians to know the facts before they make any decisions about future marital plans.

2. The care of the woman (7:34)

There is a difference[17] between the concerns of the single woman and the wife. The unmarried woman is free to dedicate totally her physical and spiritual energy to the service of God. Again, the word "holy" means "to be set apart." There is no indication anywhere in Scripture that a virgin is inherently more spiritual or righteous than a married woman. A virgin simply can devote more time and effort to spiritual exercise because she has no binding obligations to others. Contrariwise, the wife must give attention to those necessary areas which will please her husband.

3. The reasons for this counsel (7:35)

Four reasons are given. First, Paul was concerned about their spiritual development and their physical and social welfare in the midst of their circumstances. Second, he had no intention of frustrating their marital plans or expectations (the "snare"). Since the snare was a rope trap (noose or slip knot) used in hunting, he meant that he did not want to capture or constrain them. Third, he wanted them to have a comely (or beautiful) life and spiritual experience. Fourth, he did not want their Christian service to be encumbered with daily, mundane cares. He wanted them to be like Mary, sitting at the feet of Jesus, rather than like Martha, working in the kitchen (Luke 10:30–42).

---

[17]The critical Greek text places the verb translated "there is difference" (*memeristai*) at the end of verse 33. The meaning then would be that the married man is divided in his concerns and in his investment of time and effort.

VII. FATHER OF A VIRGIN (7:36–38)

What is the relationship of the "man"[18] to "his virgin"? Some have suggested that this was a spiritual marriage in which the legally married partners agreed not to have sexual intimacies but rather to live like brother and sister. Others feel that the passage is descriptive of an engaged couple.[19] The most acceptable view which fits the context and the cultural customs of that day is that the passage is dealing with a virgin and her parental guardian.[20]

A. He Can Give Her (7:36)

If certain conditions are met, it is not a sin for a father to make marital arrangements for his daughter. He must be convinced that he is not doing the proper thing by her in failing to provide for her marriage. She must be at a marriageable age. According to Plato, the "flower" of a woman's life was twenty years. She is therefore well into the fruit- or child-bearing period rather than a mere child. She must want to be married ("and need so require"). He must also want her to get married ("what he will").

B. He Can Keep Her (7:37)

Under other conditions, it is also not a sin for a father not to make such marital arrangements for his daughter. He must have a firm conviction that it is God's will for her to remain single ("standeth stedfast in his heart"). Both the father and the daughter must agree that there is no sexual or social necessity for her to get married. He must have arrived at his decision by himself and not by any external pressure.

C. He Has a Choice (7:38)

This decision must also be viewed against the background of

[18]The word for "man" does not appear in the Greek text. Rather, it is the translation of the indefinite pronoun *tis*.

[19]This can be seen in the following Bible versions: Revised Standard Version, New English Bible, and Weymouth's translation.

[20]This is seen in the King James Version and in the New American Standard Bible. It is also held by Boyer, *World Like Ours*, p. 82, and Morris, *Corinthians*, p. 122.

the adverse environment in Corinth. With that in mind, the parent who gives[21] his daughter in marriage does *well*, but the father who withholds his daughter does *better*. This is a social, not a moral, comparison.

VIII. WIDOWS (7:39–40)

To the widows, Paul set forth four absolute principles, followed by one statement of personal advice. First, wives are "bound" (*dedetai*) to their husbands for life (cf. 7:27). Second, death severs the marriage bond (cf. Rom. 7:2–3). Third, widows are then free to remarry (I Tim. 5:11, 14). They have a liberty of choice for their next husband. Fourth, Christian widows who choose to remarry must marry a believer ("only in the Lord").

Again, Paul's counsel to them must be viewed from the standpoint of the Corinthian distress (7:26, 28, 29). In his judgment (cf. 7:25), based upon personal experience and Spirit-guided deliberation, he thought that they would be happier if they would remain unmarried.

QUESTIONS FOR DISCUSSION

1. Does the rise in Christian marriage seminars and in the publication of Bible-oriented marital books indicate that Christian marriages are failing?

2. Why have many Christians looked upon sex (its discussion and practice) as a taboo? What can be done to overcome these prejudices?

3. Should the single life be promoted as much as the marital union? In what circumstances would it be preferred? In what circumstances would it prove awkward?

4. Have divorced and separated partners been discriminated against in evangelical churches? Can they have an effective ministry?

5. Is remarriage after divorce Biblical? Give a Biblical basis for your answer. Since the evangelical world is divided on the question, how dogmatic should a person be?

---

[21]The verb here is *gamizō* not *gameō* (7:36). This is further proof of a father-daughter relationship.

6. Have single men and single women been forced out of strategic opportunities for Christian service? Would it be preferable for a pastor to be single or married?

7. What present situations would correspond to the cause of the Corinthian distress?

7

The Principles of
Christian Liberty
I Corinthians 8 — 9

Within the next three chapters (8:1 — 11:1) Paul answered their questions about "things offered to idols." When an idol worshiper offered an animal sacrifice to his god, part of the carcass was consumed by fire upon the altar, but the rest was used in different ways. The priests often took some meat for their own personal needs. Sometimes a worshiper would host a dinner in the temple area, feeding his guests with the sacrificial meat. Or he would take some of the meat home for his family needs and for dinners to which he would invite his friends. If the animal had been offered as a general public sacrifice, much of the meat would later be sold in the market (10:25). In addition, many social functions, including community dinners, were held in the temple precincts apart from animal sacrifices.

The situation was problematic. Could a Christian buy and eat sacrificial meat sold in the market? Could he accept an invitation to a private dinner where such meat would be served? Could he attend any function held within the pagan temple precincts? The answers among the Corinthians, however, were mixed. Some of the Corinthian believers said that they could do so without violating their Christian testimony, whereas others believed it was sin to do so. Thus the church wrote to Paul about this problem.

I. THE PRINCIPLES STATED (Chap. 8)

The church wanted an unqualified Yes or No answer, but Paul replied with principles that must be applied to each specific

101

situation. In the area of morals (lying, stealing, adultery), there is a simple distinction between right and wrong. The "meat" question, however, belongs to the area of Christian liberty. The rightness or wrongness in eating such meat is not found in the meat itself or in the eating of it. Both of these are morally neutral. The question of sin is introduced by the motivation behind the eating and by the consequences produced by the eating. Thus it was that Paul had to present the principles of grace that stood in marked contrast both to a firm legalism ("Do" or "Don't") and to a selfish individualism ("Nobody can tell me what to do").

A. Knowledge Alone Is Insufficient (8:1–2)

1. Knowledge is claimed by all (8:1a)

Knowledge alone is an insufficient basis for proper behavior in the realm of Christian liberty. All Christians possess some facts in this area.[1] The believers at Corinth all knew about the uniqueness of the true God and the folly of idolatry. But they did not know how to resolve conflicts among the brethren when questions developed over the relationship of Christianity to contemporary culture. That is why they had written to the apostle for counsel. Perhaps both sides claimed to have full knowledge of the problem but remained adamant in their determination not to change their respective opinions.

2. Knowledge puffs up (8:1b)

The purpose of Christian fellowship is edification (14:12, 26; cf. Eph. 2:19–22; 4:16). Knowledge by itself simply "puffs up" the person who acts only upon what he knows (cf. 4:6). It is self-destructive (cf. blowing up of a balloon until it pops). Proud knowledge is not produced by the Holy Spirit (Gal. 5:22–23).

3. Knowledge, actually, is never complete (8:2)

A believer always can learn more about God, himself, others, or various situations. Paul thus criticized the Christian who

[1]Several commentators believe that the opening phrase ("we know that we all have knowledge") was a statement from the Corinthian letter incorporated by Paul into his answer. However, they disagree over whether Paul approved or disapproved this thesis.

thinks that he has arrived at full knowledge about any subject, especially that of Christian liberty.[2] Kay correctly observed: "Knowledge is proud that it has learnt so much. Wisdom is humble that it knows no more."[3]

B. Love Is the Proper Basis (8:3)

Love edifies both the giver and the recipient of that love (8:1b). Genuine love for God can be seen in a genuine loving concern for the spiritual welfare of God's children (I John 5:1–3). This type of love should dictate a believer's decision in the realm of Christian liberty. God will know whether brotherly love or selfish indulgence motivates a Christian's actions (8:3b). If a Christian really loves his fellow believer, he will be willing *to give to* him and *to give up for* him. To know and to love God also means to be known and to be loved by Him (cf. Gal. 4:9).

C. Knowledge Is Necessary (8:4–6)

To make valid decisions in any realm, men must know something. Interpersonal relationships cannot be immersed in ignorance. In Christian liberty, love must form the foundation, but knowledge must provide the superstructure. Paul recognized that concept and proceeded to give a series of categorical statements that all believers should know and act on.

1. An idol is nothing (8:4a)

Christians know that "an idol is nothing." It is a nonentity. An idol is an *it*, not a *him* or *her*. Idols are not living personalities. They are inanimate objects, made of wood, stone, or metal, to which deceived people have ascribed personality.

2. Only one God exists (8:4b)

They also know that only one God exists, the God who created the world and who has revealed Himself through the Scriptures. Polytheism is a myth fabricated by human superstition, whereas monotheism is real and factual. The Jewish *Shema*

---

[2]The first of the three verbs translated as "know" in this verse is a perfect tense *egnōkenai*, meaning "to achieve total knowledge."

[3]Cited by Leon Morris, *The First Epistle of Paul to the Corinthians*, p. 125.

declares, "Hear, O Israel; The Lord our God is one Lord" (Deut. 6:4). The New Testament writers accepted the emphasis of the oneness of God within the Old Testament and declared it to be a trinitarian oneness within the divine being. Christians therefore believe in one God who eternally exists as three Persons: Father, Son, and Holy Spirit (cf. Matt. 28:19).

3. Names and reality are different (8:5)

Believers know that the giving of names to pagan deities ("gods" and "lords") does not mean that those deities actually exist. In essence, those spiritually blinded people are really worshiping demons (cf. 10:19–21). When Moses said that the God of Israel was the "God of gods and Lord of lords" (Deut. 10:17), he was asserting the unique supremacy of Jehovah over the false polytheism of the pagans.

A figure of the goddess Diana of Ephesus.

4. There is one God (8:6a)

Christians know[4] that there is only one God. He is the source of all things, both physical and immaterial ("of whom are all things"), and the saved find their goal and purpose in living in Him ("we in him").[5]

5. There is one Lord (8:6b)

They know further that there is only one Lord, who is characterized in three ways. First, His name is Jesus Christ. Second, He is the agent of both the natural and the spiritual creations ("by whom," *dia*; cf. Col. 1:16). Third, through Him believing sinners have been saved ("we by him"; cf. Acts 4:12).

D. Knowledge and Love Must Work Together (8:7–13)

What a believer ought to do should take precedence over what he wants to do and what he knows he can do. He must act responsibly toward God, before the family of God, and within society (cf. 10:31–32; Rom. 14:7).

1. To be aware of the weak conscience (8:7–8)

A concerned Christian should be aware that some believers regard certain nonmoral issues to be sinful for them because of their past involvement in a sinful society (8:7).[6] At Corinth there were Christians who intensely felt that "food offered to idols" was sinful for them to eat (note the phrase "unto this hour"), and that it involved them in fellowship with false gods whom they had repudiated in their conversion.[7] The Jews and the Gentile proselytes converted out of the synagogue ministry would not

[4]The opening words, "But to us" (*all ' hēmin*), *are very emphatic in the Greek text.*

[5]The phrase "we in him" contains the preposition *eis,* better translated as "into" or "for."

[6]Some Greek manuscripts read "custom" (*synētheiai*) rather than "conscience" (*syneidēsei*). Since they had a long history of being accustomed to an idol-centered culture, they could not completely forget its influence on their lives.

[7]According to Connick, some of the pagans had the "conviction that the spirit of the gods possessed men when they ate food that had been sacrificed." C. Milo Connick, *The New Testament,* p. 278.

have had that problem with a "defiled" conscience. Hodge says that "a *weak* conscience is one which either regards as wrong what is not in fact so; or one which is not clear and decided in its judgments."[8]

A Christian should be sensitive to the fact that the exercise or the nonexercise of liberty in the nonmoral realm ("meat" or better translated as "food") does not determine one's basic spiritual condition (8:8). Elsewhere Paul wrote: "For the kingdom of God is not meat and drink; but righteousness, and peace, and joy in the Holy Ghost. For he that in these things serveth Christ is acceptable to God, and approved of men" (Rom. 14:17–18). Spirituality is caused by complete submission to the indwelling Holy Spirit and demonstrated by the production of Christian character (Gal. 5:22–23). "Meat commendeth us not to God." The idea behind "commendeth" (*parastēsei*) is "to be presented" (cf. Rom. 6:13; II Cor. 4:14); or "to be brought near" (cf. Acts 27:24). Thus, to use liberty does not make one more spiritual nor does its nonuse make one less spiritual.

2. *To honor the weak conscience (8:9–11)*

Paul warned ("take heed") the believer with the strong conscience not to exercise his right ("liberty" or "authority," *exousia*; cf. John 1:12) if it became a hindrance to the spiritual growth of the Christian with the weak conscience (8:9). He is to be a building block to his brother, not a "stumbling block" (*proskomma*). The latter refers to a stone in the path which caused a person to trip and fall. The real issue in Christian liberty is the effect that its exercise has on other people (cf. Rom. 14:13).

In his illustration (8:10–11) Paul showed how the exercise of liberty could harm a spiritual brother. A Christian who knew that there is only one God and that idols are nonentities ("thee which hast knowledge") attended a banquet within the pagan temple and ate meat from animals that had previously been sacrificed to that idol. He did not see anything wrong in his actions. However, a spiritual brother, who was a weak Christian and still believed in the reality of idols observed this action. This "brother" was "emboldened" or "edified" (*oikodomēthēsetai*) to fol-

---

[8]Charles Hodge, *Commentary on the First Epistle to the Corinthians,* p. 146.

low the example of the strong Christian. He must have reasoned that if the strong believer could do it, it must be all right. When the weak Christian ate the food, however, he felt that he had sinned because he was doing the same thing that he had done in his unsaved life. Thus, he "perished" through the indiscriminate use of liberty by the stronger brother. Paul said that all things in the nonmoral realm of liberty "are pure; but it is evil for that man who eateth with offence" (Rom. 14:20). He further added that "he that doubteth is damned ["comes under judgment," *katakekritai*] if he eat, because he eateth not of faith" (Rom. 14:23). The weak Christian "perished" in that he suffered spiritual loss, a sense of sin that affected his fellowship with God.[9]

This reckless use of liberty actually violates the purpose for which Christ died (8:11b). If Christ died to deliver men from sin, why should Christians use their freedom to lead others into sin? Also, since Christ gave up His rights when He became man (Phil. 2:5–11), should not Christians also give up their rights to help their brothers?

3. To avoid sinning against the weak conscience (8:12–13)

A Christian actually sins when he causes his brother to sin (8:12). Ultimately, a "sin against a brother" is a "sin against Christ." The Lord Jesus told Saul that the latter's persecution of the church was really against Him (Acts 9:4–5; cf. Matt. 25:40, 45). Believers are inseparable members of Christ's "body, of his flesh, and of his bones" (Eph. 5:30). Reckless use of liberty actually wounds *(typtontes)*, meaning "to strike vigorously") the weak conscience. It discourages and frustrates him; it destroys his confidence in the loving concern of others.

Christ told His disciples to remove that which offends (Matt. 5:29–30; 17:27; 18:6–9). To avoid offending his Christian brother, Paul chose not to exercise his right of eating sacrificial meat. His resolution is extremely emphatic (used the double

---

[9]The word "perish" is *apollytai*. It is used of eternal punishment (John 3:16). Boyer thinks that the weak brother is really an unsaved person, professing to be a Christian, who goes to hell through the poor example of a real Christian. James L. Boyer, *For a World Like Ours*, p. 90. S. Lewis Johnson sees it as the beginning of the sin unto death, *The Wycliffe Bible Commentary*, p. 1242.

negative *ou mē*): "I will absolutely not eat meat." He further was prepared to make it a permanent decision ("while the world standeth"). His liberty was not a life-compelling force (cf. 6:12b); rather, he controlled it so that it would never hinder the spiritual advancement of his brother. Christians today should do likewise.

II. THE PRINCIPLES ILLUSTRATED (Chap. 9)

In the closing verse of the previous chapter (8:13), Paul personally inserted himself into the solution of the problem. He was not against using himself and his experiences as illustrations. This is possible only if a person practices what he preaches. Elsewhere he wrote, "Those things, which ye have both learned, and received, and heard, and seen in me, do . . ." (Phil. 4:9).

A. Rights That Paul Did Not Use (9:1–14)

To illustrate the surrender of rights within Christian liberty, Paul chose to talk about one right that all people possess. It is the right to receive wages for work (cf. I Tim. 5:18). By moving into this noncontroversial area, Paul was free to explain clearly what he had mentioned earlier (8:9, 13).

1. *As an apostle (9:1–6)*

In a series of four questions[10] (all expecting an affirmative answer[11]), Paul proved that he was a genuine apostle possessing certain rights inherent in that office. He elsewhere claimed to be an apostle (Rom. 1:1; Gal. 1:1) and was recognized as such by other apostles (Gal. 2:7–9). He was free in that he was delivered from the bondage of sin (John 8:32, 36), in that he was under no obligation to any man (9:19), and in that he had total freedom within the realm of the nonmoral issues. An apostle had to be one who had seen the resurrected Christ and who had been commissioned by Him to preach (Acts 1:20–22); Paul fulfilled that qualification (Acts 26:13–19). Apostles laid the foundation of the church (Eph. 2:20), and Paul did that through his itiner-

[10]The first two questions are reversed in the critical text.

[11]The words translated "not" are all based on the negative *ou*. Questions using this negative suggest an affirmative answer.

ant preaching and writing ministry. He founded the church at Corinth (3:10; cf. Acts 18:1–18). The Corinthian Christians were his "work in the Lord."

Since Paul was not one of the original twelve apostles, his apostleship was often under suspicion and attack. Of all people, however, the Corinthians should have known that Paul was a legitimate apostle (8:2). After all, he was the pioneer evangelist who had opened their city to the gospel. Many of them had been personally saved and taught through his ministry. They were his seal of authentication.[12]

His critics often pointed to his refusal to be financially supported by the local church in which he was serving as an argument against his apostleship (cf. II Cor. 11:7–12). They reasoned that if Paul knew that he was a genuine apostle he would have accepted money like the other apostles did; they contended that his unwillingness to do so showed his falseness. Paul had a prepared answer[13] for such a false charge (8:3; cf. 2:15).

He had the power or right (*exousian;* same word as "liberty," 8:9) to eat and to drink food provided by the local Christians (cf. III John 5–7). He had the right to be married, to travel with his Christian wife,[14] and to have both of them supported by the churches (8:5). Apparently, this policy was followed by the other apostles (e.g., Cephas, or Simon Peter; Matt. 8:14) and by the half-brothers of Christ (e.g., James; Gal. 1:19; cf. Mark 6:3). Both Barnabas and he had the right to refrain from working with their hands to support their missionary travels (8:6; cf. Acts 18:1–3; II Thess. 3:6–10).

2. As a human being (9:7–10)

According to the natural laws of society, workers are to be paid for their labor. Three illustrations are cited (9:7). A *soldier* is not expected to pay for his own uniform, lodging, food, travel expenses, and weapons. A *farmer* who plants and cares for a vineyard has a perfect right to eat of its grapes. A *shepherd* has the right to drink the milk of the flock that he tends.

[12]The seal (*sphragis*) was an implanted mark upon clay or wax to show ownership.

[13]The word for "answer" (*apologia*) refers to a logical defense of one's position.

[14]The phrase "a sister, a wife" (*adelphēn gynaika*) is an appositive.

These human rights ("as a man," *kata anthrōpon*) are supported by divine commandment (9:8). The Bible, not cultural standards, must stand alone as the spiritual basis of faith and practice. To prove his point, Paul quoted the rights of animals, which were incorporated into the Mosaic law (9:9). An ox has the right to eat of the grain that he has trod (cf. Deut. 25:4). In a series of two questions (9:9b–10a), the apostle showed that the rights of working animals, in principle, apply to the rights of human workers. God *is* concerned about the welfare of animals (Ps. 104:14, 21, 27; Matt. 6:26), but the real intent behind the command for the humane treatment of animals was the proper reimbursement of laborers ("For our sakes, no doubt, this is written," 9:10). Paul used this same Old Testament verse to demonstrate that church elders should be given proper financial support (I Tim. 5:17–18). In conclusion, those who work at the beginning or the ending of a project (plowing or threshing) should do so with the full expectation that they will all equally share in the profits (9:10; cf. 3:6–9).

3. As a minister (9:11–14)

Paul then moved from the general principle of wages for secular work to the specific application of financial support for spiritual service. He claimed that he had the right to reap material benefits ("carnal things" refers to money, food, and lodging) since he had performed a spiritual ministry in their midst (9:11). The way in which he phrased his question (". . . is it a great thing . . . ?") shows that both he and they would agree concerning his claim of their monetary support.

The Corinthians had supported other preachers who had this right[15] and who had ministered to the church (9:12a). Since this was so, the apostle had a prior right and even greater claim on their financial assistance (note the words, "are not we rather?"). He was the one who had founded the church and who had been their first teacher; he was their spiritual father (4:15). Paul, however, willingly chose not to use his right when he pioneered the work because he did not want anyone (synagogue Jews or pagan Gentiles) to think that he was "in it for what he

---

[15]Again, the word for "power" is *exousia*, used earlier several times (8:9; 9:4–6).

could get out of it." He wanted to remove all obstacles that might throw suspicion upon the real motivation behind his ministry. He wanted people to know that he was interested in them and in their spiritual welfare only, and not in their purses.

Regardless of whether they were saved out of Judaism or paganism, the Corinthians should have known that all ministers have the right to be supported (9:13). The Levitical attendants who worked in the tabernacle, in the Solomonic temple, and in the Zerubbabel-Herod temple gained their livelihood from the tithes and offerings stored within the temple. In addition, the Aaronic priests were able to eat part of the animals that were sacrificed on the altar (Lev. 7:6, 8–10, 28–36; Num. 18:8–24). The pagan priests were likewise supported by the sacrificial gifts of the idolatrous worshipers.

In analogy ("even so"), Jesus Christ had charged that gospel preachers in this age should draw their personal and family subsistence from their respective ministries (9:14). Priests live "out of" (ek) the temple and preachers are to live "out of" the gospel. In His ordination address to the seventy, Christ said: "And in the same house remain, eating and drinking such things as they give: for the laborer is worthy of his hire" (Luke 10:7; cf. I Tim. 5:18).

B. Reasons Why Paul Did Not Use His Rights (9:15–18)

1. His motivation (9:15)

Since Paul had the right, why did he not use it (cf. 9:12)? He had not asked for money from the Corinthians when he originally evangelized their city, nor did he want the church to think that he was now asking for monetary support (9:15a). He firmly believed that if he forced people to pay for his services, then the motivation behind his preaching would be questioned (9:15b).

2. His responsibility (9:16)

He recognized that God had given him the awesome responsibility to preach and that he had to preach without giving any thought to financial support (9:16). Paul was not free to preach or not to preach; it was his debt (Rom. 1:15; II Cor. 5:11). Rather, he was free not to take offerings.

3. His reward (9:17–18)

The apostle knew that he would receive a reward, or wages (*misthon;* same as "hire" in Luke 10:7), from God if he performed his task willingly apart from any earthly praise or remuneration (9:17a). Peter told the elders the same truth: "Feed the flock of God which is among you, taking the oversight thereof, not by constraint, but willingly; not for filthy lucre, but of a ready mind" (I Peter 5:2). Such faithful pastors will receive a crown of glory (I Peter 5:4). Paul also recognized that he had to preach even when he felt unwilling because God had entrusted him with the gospel ministry (9:17b; cf. I Tim. 1:11–12). Stewards have to do what their masters want them to do even when they are tired and when they do not like the task assigned to them (cf. 4:1–2).

He knew that his reward involved the preaching of the gospel at no cost to his listeners (9:18a). To him, eternal life was a gift and so was his preaching. Someone has said, "His pay was to do it without pay!" Thus, Paul did not want to abuse his right of financial support ("my power in the gospel") by demanding to be paid for his services (9:18b).

C. Rights That Paul Did Use (9:19–27)

Paul was free (9:1). He was free to do what he wanted to do, and what he wanted most to do was to glorify God and be a blessing to others. He had the right to give up the use of his rights, or he could elect to exercise his rights. The choice was his.

1. Right to serve (9:19–21)

To the Galatians Paul wrote, "For, brethren, ye have been called unto liberty; only use not liberty for an occasion to the flesh, but by love serve one another" (Gal. 5:13). Paul did just that. Even though no man held any formal obligation over him, he chose to regard himself as the slave of all men to gain their salvation and to encourage their Christian growth (9:19). Like Christ, he did not want to be served, but rather to serve (Matt. 20:28). He did this both for the sake of men (9:19) and for the sake of the gospel (9:23).

Specifically, Paul accommodated his life-style and his methodology of presentation to the group he was trying to reach with the gospel. He did not alter his message or his morals. He was both firm and flexible at the same time. To reach the Jew, he was willing to preach in the synagogues on the Sabbath. He chose to have Timothy, who was half Jew and half Greek, circumcised that the missionary team might have maximum effectiveness (Acts 16:3). As a testimony to the Jerusalem Jews, he submitted to the request to identify himself with Jews who had taken a vow of purification (Acts 21:20–26).

The phrases "them that are under the law" and "them that are without law" (9:20–21) refer to the Jews and the Greeks. In Christian experience, the two groups could refer to those who were legalistic in their behavior and to those who recognized no legal code in the area of Christian liberty. The apostle, however, tempered his statement by saying that he was always under the moral law of God as an obedient slave of Christ (9:21b).

2. Right to be flexible (9:22–23)

Paul always considered the brother with the weak conscience (9:22; cf. 8:9, 10, 13) and adjusted his own behavior accordingly. This is the main thrust of this section.

The apostle claimed the right to be flexible (9:22b). He sought to win men to Christ where he found them. Christ did the same thing. In personal conversation, He approached the Jewish ruler Nicodemus much differently than He did the Samaritan woman (John 3; cf. John 4). Likewise Paul was pliable, using his rights at one time and not using them on other occasions. Just as Christ surrendered the independent exercise of his divine rights in His condescension to servanthood to achieve the salvation of men (Phil. 2:5–11), so Paul willingly gave up the exercise of his rights[16] to share in the very essence of the gospel message (9:23).

3. Right to excel (9:24–27)

Next to the Olympic games, the Isthmian games held at Corinth every three years were the most highly acclaimed athlet-

---

[16]Paul did not give up his rights, only the exercise of those rights. Christ did not give up His divine rights when He became man, only the independent exercise of them. He did use His divine rights, but only within the will of God for His incarnate life.

The stadium at Delphi, Greece.

ic contests of the first century. To compete, an athlete had to have Greek citizenship. Paul saw in the games an excellent analogy to the Christian life. To him, life was like a race. To compete, a person had to be a regenerated Christian. The reward for running was not heavenly citizenship, but the praise of the Savior at the judgment seat of Christ. To win this reward, Paul determined to give up the exercise of some of his rights to achieve excellence in his life and ministry.

In the Olympic and Isthmian games, there could be only one winner among the many participants in any given race (9:24a). In the Christian life, however, all believers are participants and all can be winners. In the physical contest men compete against others, but in the spiritual race a man competes against himself as he obeys or disobeys the will of God for his life. Thus, a believer should have the motivation to win (9:24b). Christianity is not a spectator sport.

Everyone who strives or agonizes (*agōnizomenos*) to win goes through a strict training program before the race (9:25). As the athlete prepared for the games with strenuous exercise, proper diet and sleep, and mental concentration to gain a "corruptible" pine wreath placed upon his head, should not the believer discipline himself to win an incorruptible crown (9:25b)? In contrast to the corruptible crown given for self-mastery, four spiritual rewards are mentioned in the Scriptures: the crown of rejoicing for faithful witnessing (I Thess. 2:19); the crown of righteousness for loving the coming of Christ (II Tim. 4:8); the crown of life for enduring trials (James 1:12); and the crown of glory for faithfully pastoring churches (I Peter 5:4).

Paul, then, saw himself as a Christian runner with a definite goal guiding his life (9:26). He did not see himself as a shadow boxer; rather, he saw his Christian life as a fight and victory to be gained over sin, flesh, and Satan. Near to martyrdom, he could shout triumphantly: "I have fought a good fight, I have finished my course, I have kept the faith" (II Tim. 4:7). He sensed a tremendous responsibility to minister to himself and to keep himself in the will of God, lest, in preaching to others, God would detect flaws in him and remove him from the ministry (9:27). The word "castaway" literally means "disapproved" (*adokimos*). An Olympic athlete who won a race did not lose his Greek citizenship if he was subsequently disqualified; however, he did lose the honor and forfeited his wreath crown. Christians, like Paul, should not want to lose the opportunity to serve Christ and the subsequent praise at the judgment seat of Christ (cf. 3:14–15).

QUESTIONS FOR DISCUSSION

1. What contemporary cultural practices correspond to the issue of things offered to idols? What about movie attendance, dancing, card playing, and watching television indiscriminately?

2. How can a weak Christian become strong? Can a strong Christian ever become weak?

3. Does God give and take away liberty as a Christian matures? As he moves to another locality?

4. Why do Christians so often disagree over the rightness and the wrongness of nonmoral issues?

5. Should churches or Christian colleges adopt codes of conduct within the area of Christian liberty? Is this legalistic?

115

6. How can Christians have a greater ministry to Jews? to the inner city? to minorities?

7. How can Christians achieve excellence in their lives and ministries? What causes them to be content with their mediocrity?

8

The Violation of Liberty
I Corinthians 10:1 — 11:1

The possession and awareness of liberty do not guarantee success. History records cases of the deliverance of peoples from oppression only to be led into a different type of bondage.[1] A person can be set free from the will of another and then become a slave of his own will. Paul recognized that Christian liberty could likewise be misused.

I. BY ISRAEL (10:1-15)

The connective "moreover" (*gar,* usually translated as "for") joins Paul's fear of disapproval (9:27) with an illustration of failure from Israel's past. Paul constantly exercised self-discipline so that he would not forfeit the rights and privileges of his apostleship. Israel, however, failed to discipline herself. Shortly after her deliverance from Egyptian bondage, she behaved in such a way that she merited God's disapproval. She did not lose her covenant relationship to God (Rom. 11:1-2, 28), but she did surrender the joys and rights of her political freedom.

Someone has said that those who are ignorant of history are bound to repeat it. Paul did not want the Corinthians to repeat the sins that the Israelites committed during their wanderings from Egypt to Canaan (10:1a).

A. The Position of All (10:1-4)

In this section, Paul used the word "all" (*pantes*) five times.

[1]Poland went from the control of Hitler's Germany to that of communist Russia.

117

Thus, he emphasized the unity of the people. Just as all Christians are equally saved and possess the same justified standing before God (Gal. 5:26–28), so all the Israelites shared in the national redemption from Egypt.

1. They all were under the cloud (10:1b)

Israel had the guarantee of God's presence, protection, and guidance in the visible cloud. Moses wrote, "And the Lord went before them by day in a pillar of a cloud, to lead them the way; and by night in a pillar of fire, to give them light; to go by day and night: He took not away the pillar of the cloud by day, nor the pillar of fire by night, from before the people" (Exod. 13:21–22; cf. Num. 14:14).

2. They all passed through the sea (10:1c)

With the water in front, mountains on both sides, and the pursuing Egyptians behind, the plight of the Israelites was desperate. They were unable to save themselves, but God sent a wind to separate the Red Sea when Moses stretched out his hand upon the waters. What followed was one of the most dramatic moments of history: "And the children of Israel went into the midst of the sea upon the dry ground: and the waters were a wall unto them on their right hand, and on their left" (Exod. 14:22). Subsequently, the Egyptians drowned when the sea walls collapsed upon them. This event marked the supernatural redemption of the Israelites.

3. They all were baptized (10:2)

Baptism signifies a believer's identification with Christ in His death and resurrection and publicly manifests a death to the old life and a desire to walk in newness of life (Rom. 6:3–4). In a sense, the Israelites experienced baptism. They were completely immersed — the sea floor was under them, the sea walls on either side of them, and the cloud above them. The purpose of their baptism was to show their complete break with their old life of Egyptian bondage and their anticipation of blessings as free men. In the baptism in the Holy Spirit, believers are baptized both into Christ (Gal. 3:27) and into the true church, the mystical body of Christ (12:13). They have a common unity in their recognition of their divine leader and Savior. So it was with Israel. Separate individuals were forged into one nation under the supernaturally appointed leader, Moses.

4. *They all ate the spiritual meat (10:3)*

The psalmist called it "angels' food" (Ps. 78:25). For forty years, God nourished them with daily[2] manna to relieve their hunger. This manifested their participation in the supernatural provision of food. It was "spiritual" both because of its heavenly origin and its spiritual significance. In the Sermon on the Bread of Life, Christ contrasted Himself with the manna: ". . . Moses gave you not that bread from heaven; but my Father giveth you the true bread from heaven. For the bread of God is he which cometh down from heaven, and giveth life unto the world" (John 6:32–33). He clearly identified Himself: "I am the bread

---

[2]No manna fell on the Sabbath. On the sixth day, they were to gather twice the daily quota to carry over into the Sabbath (Exod. 16:4–5).

The rugged terrain in the area of Mount Sinai.

of life" (John 6:35; cf. 6:48, 51). Just as the eating of the manna
gave temporary, physical life, so the eating of Christ (believing
and receiving Him) brings eternal, spiritual life.

5. They all drank the water (10:4)

When the Israelites arrived at Rephidim, they complained
because there was no water to drink (Exod. 17:1). At the instruction of God, Moses smote the designated rock and water
miraculously came out of it (Exod. 17:5–6). They all shared in
the supernatural provision for thirst. It was spiritual drink in
that it typified Jesus Christ,[3] who was smitten on the cross to
provide the waters of everlasting life (John 4:14; 6:35; 7:37–39).

How did the rock follow them? An early Jewish legend claims
that the rock literally followed them. It may mean that the water
followed them as it flowed down the dry river beds alongside
where they walked (cf. Ps. 105:41). It could also mean that the
"spiritual rock," namely Christ, was with them at all times in their
wanderings.

B. The Punishment of Many (10:5–6)

"But" the adult generation of Israelites that was redeemed
out of Egyptian bondage never enjoyed the blessings of Canaan.
At Kadesh-Barnea, they refused to enter out of fear of the in-
habitants and out of unbelief in God's promise (Num. 14; cf.
Heb. 3:7–19). For these sins and others, they were so judged by
God that they lived and died in the wilderness during the next
forty years. The word here translated "overthrown" literally
means "to spread out." Wherever they wandered, the wilderness
was covered with the graves and corpses of the disobedient
(Num. 14:29). God was pleased with their covenant position in
the fathers (Abraham, Isaac, and Jacob), but He was "not
pleased" with their practice.

Paul saw a clear analogy between the experience of the Israelites and that of contemporary Christians (10:6). They were
"examples" or types (typoi). One purpose of reading Old Testa-

[3]Christ is clearly seen as the rock (10:4; cf. Matt. 16:18; I Peter 2:6–8). Since
Jehovah is depicted as the rock (Deut. 32:15; Ps. 18:2), this identification is a
further proof of Christ's deity.

ment history is to learn how to avoid the sins of the past.

C. The Practice of Some (10:7–10)

This section is easily divided by the fourfold use of the word "neither" (*mēde*) followed by four commands.[4] It specially shows those evil things which brought about the severe chastisement of the Israelites (cf. 10:6).

1. Idolatry (10:7)

Israel involved herself in the very idol festivals that marked the Egyptian polytheism when she erected the golden calf. Her eating, drinking, and playing (dancing) were pagan practices. To do such things even in the name of Jehovah was absolutely wrong. The Corinthian predicament was practically parallel. Some Christians thought that they could attend a feast dedicated to the idols in the pagan temple and eat the food that had been sacrificed to the false gods without being defiled. Paul said that this attitude and this action were wrong and forbidden (cf. 8:10; 10:20–21). "Neither be ye" literally means "stop becoming" (*ginesthe*). This means that some of the Corinthians were constantly going to pagan festivals in the temple.

2. Fornication (10:8)

Moses wrote: "And Israel abode in Shittim, and the people began to commit whoredom with the daughters of Moab. And they called the people unto the sacrifices of their gods: and the people did eat, and bowed down to their gods" (Num. 25:1–2). This fornication included intermarriage with the pagans and also premarital and extramarital sexual relationships with them. The apostle had earlier warned against this misuse of the believer's body (6:9–20). Such sexual sin, both real and imagined, is a direct result of intimate involvement in the practices of a pagan society. In fact, it was Balaam ". . . who taught Balak to cast a stumblingblock before the children of Israel, to eat things sacrificed unto idols, and to commit fornication" (Rev. 2:14; cf.

---

[4]The first and fourth commands are second person plural imperatives, whereas the middle two (second and third) are first person plural hortatory subjunctives.

2:20). The judgment for this sin produced physical death for thousands of Israelites (cf. Num. 25:9).[5]

3. Tempting the Lord (10:9)

Men tempt God when they show their dissatisfaction with His gracious provision of protection and of the basic necessities of life. The Israelites complained about their lack of food and water (Exod. 17:1–7; Num. 21:5–6). They thought that their past life in Egypt with its appropriate diet had some advantages over their liberated state. Because of this sin, "much people" died through the poisonous snake bites (Num. 21:6). The remedy was to look in faith at the brass serpent which pictured Christ on the cross (John 3:14–15). Christians should do the same thing when they have an inclination to complain.

4. Murmuring (10:10)

Although the Israelites had persistently committed the trespass of murmuring, Paul may have referred to their disenchantment with the leadership of the divinely appointed Moses (Num. 14:2, 36; 16:11, 41). The rebellion led by Korah dramatically ended when the opened earth swallowed the rebels (Num. 16). The application of this admonition to the Corinthians is not entirely clear. In the area of Christian liberty, however, there are many who do not want to listen to the counsel of the church's leaders; they want to guide their own lives. This can only bring ruin.

D. The Purposes of History (10:11–15)

Again, Paul pointed out the fact that the past experiences of the Israelites were examples of Christian living (10:11a; cf. 10:6). Valuable spiritual lessons can be learned and applied from their virtues and vices. In fact, the apostle listed five such purposes.

1. To admonish men (10:11)

Parents can bring their children up "in the nurture and ad-

[5]There is no numerical discrepancy. In one day, twenty-three thousand perished (10:8), but the total number who died was twenty-four thousand (Num. 25:9), including those who were slain by the judges.

monition [*nouthesian*; same word] of the Lord" (Eph. 6:4) by challenging them from the Old Testament as well as from the New Testament. Heretics are to be rejected after two admonitions (Titus 3:10). The force of "admonition" is warning and correction designed to change past behavior and to introduce new patterns of life. Believers of this church age are those "upon whom the ends of the world ["ages," *aiōnōn*] are come." Fortunately, they can be the recipients of all the spiritual lessons from past dispensations if they are willing to learn.

2. To keep men from pride (10:12)

Basically, the lessons from history should be a warning to the Christian who places overwhelming confidence in himself and in his knowledge and exercise of liberty. There were Corinthians who convinced themselves that they could never repeat the sins of the Israelites even though they fellowshiped with pagans in the idolatrous temples. They had forgotten Solomon's counsel: "Pride goeth before destruction, and an haughty spirit before a fall" (Prov. 16:18). Without moral alertness, believers can fall from their own stedfastness (cf. II Peter 1:10; 3:17). Like Israel, they could fall short of the abundant life that God had planned for them (10:5; cf. Heb. 6:6).

3. To give men victory in testing (10:13)

The apostle pointed out that the "temptations" or tests of believers are typical human experiences ("common to man"). The Christian should rejoice when he encounters them because they are designed by God to strengthen his faith (James 1:12). God wants His children to see His faithfulness in the midst of those trials. When Jeremiah viewed the destruction of his beloved Jerusalem, he wrote: "It is of the Lord's mercies that we are not consumed, because his compassions fail not. They are new every morning; great is thy faithfulness" (Lam. 3:22–23). Also, no test will be greater than a believer's ability to bear the test ("above that ye are able"). In addition to the trial, God provides the "way of escape" (*ekbasin*). This word was used of sailors lightening their ship in the midst of a storm by throwing overboard weighty cargo (Acts 27:18, 38). In order to endure a test rather than to be sunk by it, believers will be shown by God what aspects of their life will have to be discarded or corrected. In all of this testing, the believer should draw closer to Christ who understands totally these trials (Heb. 2:17-18; 4:15-16).

4. *To keep men from idolatry (10:14)*

Paul tells the Corinthians to "flee idolatry." John gave the same command: "Little children, keep yourselves from idols" (I John 5:21). The command is logical and necessary, based upon Israel's failure to do so (note the strong "wherefore"; *dioper*). By going to the temple banquets, the Christian was doing just the opposite. Hodge observes: "By going to the verge of the allowable, they might be drawn into the sinful."[6]

5. *To give men discernment (10:15)*

The final purpose of history is to give moral and spiritual discernment about present problems. Paul says, "I speak as to the wise; judge ye what I say." The word for "wise" (*phronimois;* different from *sophos* in 1:20) conveys the thought of intelligent common sense. An Arabian proverb says: "He who knows and knows that he knows, he is wise; follow him." A wise Christian will accept Paul's admonition and will guide his life by it.

II. BY FELLOWSHIP WITH DEMONS (10:16-22)

In the second epistle, Paul called for absolute separation from any involvement in pagan idolatry (II Cor. 6:14 — 7:1). His commands were pointed: "Be ye not unequally yoked together with unbelievers . . . come out from among them . . . be ye separate . . . and touch not the unclean." Five reasons were given in the form of rhetorical questions: ". . . for what fellowship hath righteousness with unrighteousness? and what communion hath light with darkness? And what concord hath Christ with Belial? or what part hath he that believeth with an infidel? And what agreement hath the temple of God with idols?" (II Cor. 6:14-15).

In this present section, Paul wanted to demonstrate that participation in the pagan feasts within the temple actually was a

---

[6]Charles Hodge, *Commentary on the First Epistle to the Corinthians,* p. 183.

misuse of Christian liberty and really involved them in fellowship with the evil world of demons.

A. Eating Involves Fellowship (10:16–20a)

Just as family members fellowship daily with each other
around the dinner table, so religious eating involves the person
in communion with his own god. Paul illustrated this principle in
three ways.

1. Christians with Christ (10:16–17)

The partaking of the elements of the Christian ordinance of
the Lord's Supper involves the believer in fellowship with other
believers and with the Lord Jesus Christ Himself. Through sharing in "the cup"[7] and in "the bread," the believers manifest their
common faith and their mutual remembrance[8] of Christ's substitutionary atonement (10:16). The cup of wine represents His
shed blood and the bread symbolizes His marred body. To bless
the elements (Matt. 26:26; Mark 14:22) and to give thanks for
them (11:24; cf. Luke 22:17, 19) are synonymous actions. In
such observance, the believers share and manifest their spiritual
oneness in Christ as living members of the mystical body of
Christ, the true church (10:17; cf. 12:12–13; Eph. 4:4). No
Christian is excluded (contrast the words "we many" and "we all"
with "one body" and "one bread").

2. Israelites with Jehovah (10:18)

Both the people and the priests of Israel were involved in
fellowship with Jehovah their God when they ate the meat of the
animal which was sacrificed to Him. The Mosiac law commanded both the attending priest and the offerer to participate
in this way (Lev. 7:15; 8:31; Deut. 12:18).

---

[7]In actual sequence, the bread was shared before the cup (cf. 11:23–25), but here
the cup is mentioned first.

[8]Three major views of the ordinance prevail today. The Roman Catholic doctrine of transubstantiation claims that the bread and the wine are literally
changed into the flesh and the blood of Christ when the priest blesses the elements. The Lutheran teaching of consubstantiation claims that Christ is literally
present in the elements although they remain unchanged. Other evangelical
positions generally hold that the ordinance is a memorial supper to be shared in
remembrance of Christ.

3. Pagans with demons (10:19–20a)

Pagans are actually involved in fellowship with demons when they eat the sacrificial meat offered to their respective gods (10:19–20). Paul repeated what he had written earlier (10:19; cf. 8:4–8): Idols are nonpersonal entities and sacrificial meat is morally neutral. Thus, the pagan, when he eats such meat, is not fellowshiping with the nonexistent idol or god. The apostle then used the strong adversative "but" (*alla*) to show the real object of the pagan fellowship (10:20a). They sacrifice to demons (*daimoniois*),[9] not to real gods or to the true God (cf. Deut. 32:17). This statement disproves the theory that all men worship the same god, only using different terms and methods. Although idols actually do not exist, demons use men's affinity to worship idols to get worship for themselves. Unsaved men, totally deceived and blinded spiritually, are unaware that they are actually fellowshiping with the world of evil spirits. Consequently, idol worship is not morally neutral; it is sinful — evil — and should be avoided completely.

B. Mutual Fellowship with God and with Demons Is Impossible (10:20b–22)

Based upon the preceding section, Paul's conclusions are clear. He did not want the Corinthians to have "fellowship with demons" through participation in the pagan temple feasts (10:20b). He pointed out that it was impossible for them to have joint fellowship with Christ and His people and with demons and their worshipers (10:21a; "Ye cannot" is literally "ye are not able," *ou dynasthe*). They are not able to drink from two cups simultaneously. At the Lord's Table, the living Head of the church presides; at the temple feasts, the demons rule. Thus, Christians must be submissive only to Christ (10:21b)

When Israel fell into idolatry, God said: "They have moved me to jealousy with that which is not God; they have provoked me to anger with their vanities . . ." (Deut. 32:21). The strong Christians, by their violations of liberty, were doing the same thing. Jealousy is wounded love. By unconsciously fellowshiping

---

[9]The word "devils" is a poor translation of this word. There is only one devil (*diabolos*), Satan, but there are many demons.

THE VIOLATION OF LIBERTY

with demons, the believers committed spiritual adultery. In so doing, they were about to bring God's jealous anger and chastisement upon themselves (10:22a) God would never eat with Satan, thus they were doing what God Himself would not do. By their actions, they were manifesting that they were even stronger than God. Naturally, no believer is stronger than God.[10]

III. BY CONSCIENCE (10:23–11:1)

Many people live by the familiar axiom: "Let your conscience be your guide." However, a conscience can be controlled by the sin nature to justify wrongdoing (cf. Rom. 2:15). Some have an insensitive conscience — "seared with a hot iron" (I Tim. 4:2). Someone has said that a conscience is like faulty brakes: "Sometimes it works and sometimes it does not." Paul recognized the problem of believers governing their Christian liberty on the basis of conscience alone. Earlier, he had introduced the subject (8:7, 10, 12), but in this section, he demonstrated how the conscience must be controlled by the principles of liberty.

A. The Principles Repeated (10:23–24)

In the realm of nonmoral issues, "all things are lawful" for the believer to do (cf. 6:12; Rom. 14:14). However, that fact in itself does not give each believer the right or the permission to do it. Four governing principles are provided to give the Christian direction and wisdom for his decision. First, the believer should only use his liberty when it is expedient or profitable to do so (10:23a). Second, he should only exercise his right when both his brother and he would be edified by his action (10:23b). Later, Paul wrote: "Let all things be done unto edifying" (14:26b). The positive construction of the spiritual strength of the church is Christ's goal (Eph. 2:20–22), and so it should be for the believer.

In the third place, he should not use his liberty exclusively for his own gratification (10:24a). He should not live to please himself (cf. Rom. 15:1). Genuine love does not seek its own interest (13:5); it is not selfish. Fourth, he should use his rights

[10]The negative *mē* demands a negative answer.

127

for the benefit of his Christian brother (10:24b). Paul said that the believer should manifest the selfless mind of Christ in this way: "Look not every man on his own things, but every man also on the things of others" (Phil. 2:4). He is to bear the burdens of others (Gal. 6:2).

B. The Principles Illustrated (10:25–30)

Paul then selected three specific situations which illustrated how the principles could be applied.

1. The meat market (10:25–26)

A Christian can eat sacrificial meat that is sold in the pagan market place[11] if two conditions are met. First, if the issue of idolatry or fellowship with demons is not introduced, he is free to eat. He is not to be overscrupulous ("asking no question for conscience sake"). He should not ask about the origin of the meat, thus stirring up his conscience or that of his weak brother. Too many scruples can hurt rather than help at times.

The second condition is to recognize that the true God is the source of all food, both animal and vegetable (10:26; cf. Ps. 24:1). The pagan may think that the food comes from his idolatrous god, but the Christian knows that it has really come from the God of creation. He can follow Paul's counsel: "For every creature of God is good, and nothing to be refused, if it be received with thanksgiving: For it is sanctified by the word of God and prayer" (I Tim. 4:4–5). After the Flood, God Himself said to the human race through Noah: "Every moving thing that liveth shall be meat for you; even as the green herb have I given you all things" (Gen. 9:3).

2. The private dinner (10:27)

A Christian can eat sacrificial meat that is served to him by his unsaved host. Again, certain conditions must be met before this can be done. The feast or dinner must take place in a private home and not in a pagan temple. Sacrificial meat kept its idolatrous, demonic significance when eaten within a pagan temple, but it lost that meaning when sold in the marketplace or

---

[11]The word for "shambles" (*makellōi*) is better translated as "market."

eaten at home. The believer should attend because he wants to, not because he is forced to ("and ye be disposed to go"). Again, he can eat if the issue of idolatry is not raised by his scrupulous conscience.

3. The religious dinner (10:28–30)

A Christian should not eat sacrificial meat at a private dinner if the issue of idolatry and fellowship with gods as demons is superimposed upon the meal. Doubtless, the same principle would apply to the purchase of such sacrificial meat in the pagan market. The issue could be brought up either by the weak Christian or by any pagan observer.[12] Several reasons are given for this refusal to eat when the issue is brought up.

First, he should not eat "for his sake that showed it" (10:28b). Like Paul, believers should be concerned about winning the lost and edifying the believers. This can only be done when no offense or compromise is manifested (cf. 10:31-33). Second, he also should not eat out of concern for the conscience of the weaker brother (10:28c, 29; cf. 8:10, 12). Third, he should not eat because there are many other foods which he can enjoy which will not violate the conscience of his brother (10:28d).[13]

Fourth, he should not eat because he knows that his liberty will be judged by the effects of his action upon the conscience of his weak brother and not that upon his own (10:29). This concept can also be applied to the conscience of the unsaved person who observes the strong Christian. The question can be phrased in this way: "For what advantage [hinati] can there be in my liberty being judged?" Liberty was given to help and not to hinder. It was designed for the believer's enjoyment (I Tim. 6:17) and not for his criticism.

Fifth, he should not eat when his brother or the unsaved might speak evil of him or of his exercise of liberty (10:30). Even though he thanked God for the food (cf. I Tim. 4:4–5), he will still be condemned by others who see in that action a moral and a

---

[12]Note the words "If any man." The qualifying phrase used earlier ("of them that believe not," 10:27) does not appear here.

[13]The closing phrase of this verse (cf. 10:26) is not found in the critical Greek text. Regardless, the truth of the above statement stands.

doctrinal compromise. Elsewhere the apostle advised: "Let not then your good be evil spoken of" (Rom. 14:16).

C. The Principles Commanded (10:31–11:1)

In concluding this extensive section on the subject of Christian liberty (8:1 — 11:1), Paul issued three simple commands.

1. Do everything for the glory of God (10:31)

The word "all" encompasses not only the realm of the non-moral issue, but every aspect of life: such as vocation, marital and family responsibilities, and use of money. Both the participation ("whether therefore ye eat or drink") and the nonparticipation ("or whatsoever ye do") in sacrificial food should have the glorification of God as its ultimate goal and reason for doing. The Westminster Catechism states: "The chief end of man is to glorify God and to enjoy Him forever." Enjoyment logically follows, not precedes, glorification.

2. Give no offense (10:32–33)

Paul charged: "Let us not therefore judge one another any more: but judge this rather, that no man put a stumbling block or an occasion to fall in his brother's way" (Rom. 14:13). No believer should make himself an obstacle to the salvation of any sinner or to the edification of any saint. In this verse, the word "Jews" refers to the unsaved Jews, the title "Gentiles" applies to the unsaved Gentiles, and the phrase "church of God" incorporates both saved Jews and saved Gentiles within the mystical body of Christ (cf. Matt. 16:18; Acts 20:28).

Paul did not ask them to do anything that he had not done (10:33). He was totally concerned with others. Although he did not accommodate his message to please men (cf. Gal. 1:10), he did seek their spiritual pleasure or welfare. He was burdened over their "profit,"[14] not his own. He wanted them to be saved.

3. Be followers of Paul (11:1)

It is not wrong to follow a man *if* that man is following Christ. Paul was! Paul followed Christ in that he willingly gave up the

---

[14]This is the same word previously translated as "expedient" (cf. 10:23).

exercise of his rights in order to gain the spiritual benefit of others. He also wrote: "For even Christ pleased not himself; but, as it is written, the reproaches of them that reproached thee fell on me" (Rom. 15:3). When Christ became man to die for the sin of man, He gave up His right to be served in order to serve (Phil. 2:5–8). Paul wanted his followers to be humble, selfless servants also.

QUESTIONS FOR DISCUSSION

1. Should more sermons be preached from the Old Testament? How can they be applied to contemporary living?

2. To what extent should Christ be seen in the Old Testament? Is He typified in every event, or only in those mentioned in the New Testament?

3. Why do some Christians fall into terrible sins? What can be done to prevent it?

4. Why do Christians resist trials which come from God? Why do they collapse when they should endure?

5. What contemporary practices will involve believers in fellowship with demons? How about transcendental meditation? the occult?

6. What present foods or practices correspond to the sacrificial food? Should a Christian watch a movie on television that he would not view in a theater? Defend your answer.

7. Do Christians really understand the principles of liberty? Are they more inclined to legalism or to licentiousness?

9

The Order of the
Local Church
I Corinthians 11:2–34

In the preceding passage Paul discussed private, personal matters (7:1 — 11:1); but in this section, he moves into problems dealing with the public worship services of the local church: the deportment of men and women (11:2–16), the abuse of the Lord's Table (11:17–34), and the function of spiritual gifts (12:1 — 14:40). Although this particular section falls within the subjects introduced by their letter to him (cf. 7:1), Paul did not use the familiar phrase ("now concerning," *peri de* as he did in 7:1, 25; 8:1; 12:1) to show his transition from one topic to another. It is possible that the matters he is about to discuss were mentioned in their letter, but it is more plausible that he had heard about these problems through the oral report of the Corinthian ambassadors (note "I hear," 11:18; cf. 1:11; 16:17). They are related to both the preceding and the following sections. The self-assertion of some women within the church serves as another example of the misuse of rights and liberty, whereas the nature of the Lord's Table had been previously mentioned (cf. 10:16). Both problems doubtlessly influenced the abuse of spiritual gifts: the public speaking of women is singled out (14:34–35); love and edification should mark the services (13:1–13; 14:26); and order, not confusion, should guide the worship (14:33, 40).

I. THE RELATIONSHIP BETWEEN MEN AND WOMEN (11:2–16)

Paul praised the church in two areas. First, they remembered him in all things. They appreciated the apostle and attempted to observe the directions that he had given them for public worship. There was no need for him to defend his apostleship or his actions.[1]

Second, they kept the "ordinances" (*paradoseis*) which he had delivered (*paredōka*)[2] to them. The ordinances do not refer specifically to water baptism or communion, although they are included.[3] Rather, they refer to the authoritative, oral teachings given to the apostles by Jesus Christ and transmitted by them in their preaching and subsequently in their writings (cf. II Thess. 2:15). Paul delivered to men what he had received directly from Christ (cf. 11:23; 15:3). He was not dependent on the other apostles for the oral content of his message.[4] He clearly stated: "For I neither received it [the Gospel] of man, neither was I taught it, but by the revelation of Jesus Christ" (Gal. 1:12).

At Corinth, the church observed the order of worship which Paul had established in his original evangelization of the city (cf. Acts 18:1–18; "as I delivered" looks back to that time). For this, Paul could praise them; later, the apostle could not praise them for their unscriptural actions at the Lord's Table (11:17). However, the church needed further explanation *why* men and women had to dress and to act differently in the service.

A. Order of Authority (11:3)

In a series of three statements, the order of spiritual authority is absolutely established: God-Christ-man-woman. In this order, a clear distinction must be made between the equality of essence and the headship of function.

1. The head of Christ is God

The Father, Son, and Holy Spirit are equally God. The

---

[1]Later, he will be forced into this defense in his second epistle.

[2]Note that the word for "ordinances" is based upon the verbal stem for "delivered."

[3]The same word for "delivered" is used of the order for the Lord's Table (11:23).

[4]Leon Morris, however, believes that Paul received these teachings from the other apostles (*The First Epistle of Paul to the Corinthians*, p. 151).

Father is not more divine than the Son, nor is the Spirit less divine than the Son. The Father is called God (Eph. 1:3), the Son is called God (Heb. 1:8), and the Spirit is called God (Acts 5:3–4). Christ[5] claimed to be one with the Father (John 10:30), and yet He claimed that the Father was greater than all (John 10:29). In order to carry out the divine program of redemption, God sent the Son. The Son came to do the will of the Father. Thus, even though there was an equality of persons within the divine oneness, there was an order (a headship) to execute the divine counsel.

2. The head of the woman is the man

So it is in the relationship between man and woman. The man is not superior to the woman. Both are equally human and in Christ there is spiritual oneness. Paul wrote: "There is neither Jew nor Greek, there is neither bond nor free, there is neither male nor female: for ye are all one in Christ Jesus" (Gal. 3:28). However, to carry out the divine will for the family and for the church, "the man" has been established as "the head of the woman." The woman is to be submissive and obedient to her husband (Eph. 5:22; Col. 3:18; Titus 2:5).

3. The head of the man is Christ

As Christ is the head of the church, so He is "the head of every man." The man must be obedient to Christ; thus, he is commanded to love his wife even as Christ loved the church and gave Himself for it (Eph. 5:25). In fact, the man must esteem others to be better than himself (Phil. 2:3), and that includes his wife!

B. Violation of Authority (11:4–6)

1. By the man (11:4)

A man can "dishonor" Christ (his authoritative head) by praying or by prophesying with his physical head covered. Praying is when one speaks to God in behalf of man and prophesying is when one speaks to man in behalf of God (cf. 14:3). Both

---

[5]Note that the incarnate name "Christ" is used in this verse. As God who had become man, He was under the headship of God the Father.

could be either normal or extraordinary charismatic activities (1:4; cf. 12:10; 14:14). The phrase "having his head covered" literally means "having down from the head" (*kata kephalēs echōn*). It refers to the wearing of a lengthy veil or shawl, but it could also depict long hair, comparable to that of a woman.[6] In either case, the man should not seek to hide his male status by attempting to manifest his spiritual equality with the woman through outward appearance and actions. He is still a man even though there is a positional oneness. Since no discipline is offered for this violation, Paul may have included this statement only for contrast. The real problem at Corinth centered about the liberated woman.[7]

2. By the woman (11:5–6)

A woman can dishonor her husband (her "authoritative head") by praying or by prophesying with her physical head uncovered; thus, a woman could perform these spiritual ministries in the church (Philip the evangelist had four daughters who prophesied, Acts 21:8–9), but she had to do them in the right way. However, this action did not qualify her for the position of pastor or deacon. This would then place her in an authoritative position over the man which was forbidden (cf. 14:34–35; I Tim. 2:12). The "veil" was a cultural sign of subordination. By removing it, the woman admitted that her husband was her head in the family but not in the church. In a sense, she was trying to manifest her spiritual sameness with the man ("for that is even all one as if she were shaven").

The discipline for this violation is set forth in the two imperatives: "let her also be shorn" and "let her be covered." In the first, Paul stated that if she wanted to act like a man, then let her hair be cut in a manly style. In the second, he referred to the cultural custom. If it was shameful or embarrassing for a woman to have short hair or to be bald,[8] then let her wear the veil. Thus, culture

[6]In a footnote, the New International Version gives this alternate translation.

[7]Perhaps the woman demanded that the man wear the veil if she had to, or she decided to remove it in order to show spiritual equality.

[8]It has been suggested that both harlots and slave women were shaved as marks of humiliation.

had to dictate the punishment. A woman must be consistent. She must act and look like a woman both in the home and in the church. She cannot act like a woman in one and like a man in the other.

C. Basis of Authority (11:7-10)

The basis of authority within the home and the church can be found in the creative purposes of God for both man and woman.

1. The glory of creation (11:7)

A man should not be marked by the cultural badge of womanly subordination because "he is the image and glory of God." Mankind, including both man and woman, was created in the image of God (Gen. 1:26-27) and still bears that image in its sinful, fallen state (Gen. 5:1-3; 9:6; James 3:9). The image of God in man means that human beings are basically spirit beings, possessing intellect, emotion, and will. As God has sovereign dominion, so mankind was given dominion over the rest of creation (Gen. 1:26). However, Paul here stated that man (the male) *is* the image and glory of God. He is the pinnacle of God's creative work and because of his priority in creation he also has dominion over the woman (Gen. 3:16; I Tim. 2:12-13). The woman is "the glory of man," but not his image, in that she is the greatest creation that God could bring out of the man.

2. The priority of creation (11:8)

In the original creation, man came directly from the formed dust, not out of the womb "of the woman" (11:8a; cf. Gen. 2:7). However, Eve, the first woman, was created indirectly out of Adam (11:8b). The record states: "And the Lord God caused a deep sleep to fall upon Adam, and he slept: and he took one of his ribs, and closed up the flesh instead thereof; And the rib, which the Lord God had taken from man, made he a woman, and brought her unto the man" (Gen. 2:21-22). Later, Adam called her "woman, because she was taken out of Man" (Gen. 2:23).

THE ORDER OF THE LOCAL CHURCH

3. The purpose of creation (11:9)

The woman was created for (*dia*) the man to meet his needs of companionship and work. By himself, he could not fill the earth with his offspring (Gen. 1:28). Since none of the animals could meet man's needs of love and fellowship, God said: "It is not good that the man should be alone; I will make him an help meet for him" (Gen. 2:18).

4. The teaching of angels (11:10)[9]

It was the sin of pride or insubordination that caused Satan and his angels to sin (Isa. 14:12–14; I Tim. 3:6). Satan wanted to be like his authoritative head, God. Thus, the good angels can learn about the acceptance of authority through the voluntary subordination of women to their husbands. If the women try to be like their authoritative heads, their husbands, then a valuable lesson will not be able to be taught (cf. Eph. 3:10). The "power on her head" (literally "the right or authority," *exousian*) is the veil which symbolizes her acceptance of the headship of her husband.

D. Equality Within Authority (11:11–12)

The connective "nevertheless" (*plēn*) is very important. Paul wanted to balance the teaching of proper headship with that of equality. He pointed out this mutual need of both sexes for each other in two areas.

1. In the spiritual realm (11:11)

Both sexes must admit their spiritual oneness (Gal. 3:28), the loving headship of the man, and the willing submission of the woman. To carry out the divine mandate of bringing up children in the fear and admonition of the Lord, both parents must execute their respective responsibilities (Eph. 6:4; Titus 2:4–5). Women can have a responsible, authoritative, teaching position in the home and in the church to other women and to children (I Tim. 2:15).

[9]This difficult verse has been intepreted in several ways. The angels have been seen as good angels, evil angels, and as the pastors of the churches (cf. Rev. 1:20). Good angels are in attendance at meetings and are interested in God's program using men and women (Heb. 1:14; 12:22–23; I Peter 1:12).

2. In the physical realm (11:12)

Just as the woman came out of the man in the original creation, so every man since that event has come out of the womb of a woman in procreation. The woman needed the man to begin her existence and the man needs the woman to continue his existence.

In both areas, man and woman must recognize that they are equally under the authority of God who is the source of both their physical and spiritual lives ("but all things of God").

E. Propriety Within Authority (11:13–15)

Three observations are made concerning the relationship of outward appearance to the question of headship and subordination.

1. The veiling of women (11:13)

It is not proper for a woman to pray in church with her physical head unveiled. The word "comely" (*prepon*) refers to that which corresponds to the fitness of things. Thus, Paul appealed to their common sense and to the cultural custom of their day ("Judge in yourselves"). Since the veil was the mark of marriage and subordination to the husband, it was only proper that she manifest her recognition of order and headship within the church.

2. The hair of men (11:14)

It is improper for a man to have long hair, equal in length to that of a woman and that which is expected of her. The word translated "shame" (*atimia*) literally means "without honor." In his argumentative question, which demands an affirmative answer, [10] the apostle appealed to nature or to the observance of natural law. The veil is consistent with nature. A woman who has long hair, hair which drops down from the head to at least the shoulders, wears the veil which likewise reaches from the head to the shoulders; the man who has short hair should not let his hair drop to the shoulders, nor should he wear a veil that covers his complete head length. God wants men to look like men and

[10]The negative *oude* is the basis of this conclusion.

women to appear as women. In the first century, some Spartans and philosophers had long hair, but this was contrary to common practice.[11]

3. The hair of women (11:15)

It is "a glory" for a woman to have long hair. The length, color, and style of a woman's hair have always been admired by other women and men. In addition, it serves as her "covering" (literally, "instead of a covering"; *anti peribolaiou*).[12] Her hair, by going around her head, removes the need of a turban or hat in harsh weather. Since the long hair is her glory, she should veil what she glories in when she is in the presence of God within the church.

F. Resistance of Authority (11:16)

Paul expected resistance to his teaching, doubtless an outgrowth of the false application of the principles of liberty (chaps. 8 — 10). A contentious person is literally "one who loves strife" (*philoneikos*), one who battles over the meaning of words and prolongs an argument indefinitely. To that person, man or woman, who rejected the expression of headship through outward appearance, the apostle pointed out that the rebel's opposition was contrary to apostolic custom and to the practice of local churches elsewhere. As cultural customs change, the expression of subordination, whatever it is, within the church must remain constant.[13]

II. THE LORD'S SUPPER (11:17–34)

The transition between the two sections can be seen in the contrast between the two phrases: "Now I praise you" (11:2) and

[11]Vincent remarked: "In the sculptures of the catacombs the women have a close-fitting head-dress, while the men have the hair short" (cited by A. T. Robertson, *Word Pictures in the New Testament,* 4:162).

[12]This is a different word for "covering" than the word translated as "covered" or "uncovered" in the other verses.

[13]Boyer believes that contemporary women should be taught the meaning of the veil and that this practice should be carried out today; see James Boyer, *For a World Like Ours,* p. 103. Johnson sees this practice as "the ideal"; see *The Wycliffe Bible Commentary,* p. 1248.

"Now . . . I praise you not" (11:17). The subject of the ordinance of the Lord's Supper had been briefly introduced before (cf. 10:16–21).

A. The Criticism of Paul (11:17–22)

The purpose of the preacher is clear: "Preach the word . . . reprove, rebuke, exhort with all longsuffering and doctrine" (II Tim. 4:2). Correction and constructive criticism are necessary. So Paul's declaration was an authoritative command.

1. The church was divisive (11:17–19)

The church of Corinth deserved no praise for its observance of the ordinance of the Lord's Supper. Instead of receiving spiritual profit from the service, the believers were worse off for their attendance (11:17). The results contradicted the very purpose of the meeting (cf. Acts 2:42–47; Heb. 10:24–25).

The meeting was marked by "divisions" (literally "schisms," schismata; cf. 1:10; 11:18). This fact had been reported to Paul (note "I hear") and was partially accepted by him. He believed the general validity of the communication even though he realized that the charges might be partial or biased (cf. I Thess. 5:21). The phrase "first of all" indicated Paul's primary concern and should be contrasted with "the rest" (11:34b).

Their meeting together was also characterized by "heresies" (haireseis, 11:19). The word comes from a verbal root emphasizing the concept of choice. Thus, a group was given the title of "sect" or "heresy" when it was known for its commitment to certain opinions or beliefs. It is used of the Sadducees (Acts 5:17), of the Pharisees (Acts 15:5), and attributed to the Christians by the Jews (Acts 24:5, 14). However, in this context, it is clearly an expression of the sin nature (cf. Gal. 5:20). Just as fire burns away the dross to reveal the pure, Paul reasoned that the Corinthian problem did produce one favorable result. It was now easier to distinguish the false from the true (cf. I John 2:19). Those who were examined and "approved" of God (hoi dokimoi; cf. I Thess. 2:4, same word translated as "allowed" and "trieth") were believers who loved Christ and who wanted the church to prosper spiritually. The self-centered members could not readily be identified.

140

2. The church was selfish (11:20–21)

The church was selfish in both attitude (11:20) and action (11:21). The observance of the Lord's Supper should be marked by humility, selflessness, and sharing; however, their services manifested just the opposite. Note Paul's clever use of the phrases "the Lord's supper" and "his own supper" to show that contrast.

Since Christ ate the Passover dinner with His disciples before He instituted the ordinance, the early church continued that practice by eating an evening meal (often referred to as a "love feast") together before the Lord's Supper was observed (cf. II Peter 2:13; Jude 12).[14] However, just as the disciples came together into the upper room for the wrong reasons (e.g., pride, argument over greatness), so the Corinthians congregated for selfish ends. They brought their own food and either ate it before other believers arrived or ate it in the presence of the poor and of the slaves who brought nothing. Such actions showed a respect of persons and a lack of love (cf. James 2). The intent of the Lord's Supper is to produce unity and sharing; but they treated this occasion as any common meal, and yet worse than that, because hospitable courtesy was lacking.

3. The church was shameful (11:22)

In a series of five questions,[15] Paul rebuked their behavior. The purpose of the love feast and/or the Lord's Supper was not to satisfy their stomach's desire for food and drink. The church is designed to fulfill spiritual hunger; the dinner in private homes should meet physical needs. In Christ, the rich and the poor have spiritual equality, but the rich Corinthians despised the very meaning of the church of God — the fact that it is one body. They shamed the poor with their selfishness and partiality. In a concluding statement, Paul ended with a rebuke.[16] This

---

[14]Some groups (e.g., Grace Brethren) observe the practice of the evening meal as a church ordinance. Such services include foot washing, the meal, and the Lord's Supper. The meal has been called the *Agapē* or the love feast.

[15]The critical Greek text has four, omitting the brief "what?"

[16]The words "in this" can be taken either with the preceding question or with the following conclusion.

section begins and ends with his declaration: "I praise you not" (11:17; cf. 11:22).

B. The Command of Christ (11:23–26)

The problems of the love feast were carried over by the Corinthians into the observance of the Lord's Table. Problems are people, and the same people were there. This section should be contrasted with the three synoptic accounts of the institution of this event (Matt. 26:26–29; Mark 14:22–25; Luke 22:17–20).

1. Its transmission (11:23a)

Paul received[17] the instructions concerning the meaning and the observance of the ordinance directly from Christ. Even though he was not in the upper room with the eleven apostles, he denied that he was indebted to them for his knowledge of the event (cf. Gal 1:1, 12). On several occasions, Christ revealed Himself directly to Paul (Acts 9:1–16; 18:9; 22:18; 23:11; 27:23–25; II Cor. 12:7; Gal. 1:12; 2:2), and during at least one of them, the nature of the ordinance was given. As a faithful steward, Paul then delivered (paredoka, cf. 11:2) the ordinance to the Corinthians after they were converted (cf. Acts 18:1–18).[18]

2. Its nature (11:23b–25)

The ordinance was instituted and first observed on the night before Christ's crucifixion and right after Judas left the upper room to set up the arrest of the Lord.[19] Thus, it is for the Lord and for His people only.[20]

The proper order is the bread before the cup. The suffering of His body preceded the shedding of His blood. In a sense, the

[17]The fact that Paul used this word only of the Lord's Table and not for the love feast shows that only the former was commanded as a church ordinance.

[18]The verb, however, can be seen as an epistolary aorist (cf. 5:9). If so, the transmission occurred twice when he preached and when he wrote.

[19]The Greek word translated as "betrayed" (paredideto) is from the same verbal root as "delivered."

[20]If foot washing and the love feast were designed as ordinances, then the unsaved, like Judas, should be allowed to participate.

bread represents His incarnation which naturally occurred before His crucifixion, symbolized by the cup.

Christ's actions were four: He took bread (large piece of unleavened bread), He gave thanks, He broke it, and He spoke. His commands were three simple directives: "Take . . . eat . . . and do."[21] In such observance they were to remember Him: His person and His redemptive work. Thus, the bread represented His incarnate body offered on the cross for them.[22]

His actions were the same when He introduced the cup (11:25). The cup (or wine) symbolized the establishment of the new covenant in His shed blood (cf. Heb. 9:16–28). Matthew and Mark emphasized the blood ("This is my blood," Matt. 26:28; Mark 14:24) whereas Paul and Luke stressed the covenant ("This is the new covenant," 11:25; cf. Luke 22:20). God had promised Israel that a new covenant would replace the old (Jer. 31:31–37; Ezek. 36:24–28).

3. Its continuation (11:26)

Based upon revelation and divine illumination, Paul pointed out that the meaning of the observance is more important than its frequency of practice. He did not say that it should be done "often," but rather that the truth of the crucifixion is proclaimed whenever they observe it ("as often as," *hosakis*). Although it is true that the early church in Jerusalem probably practiced it daily (Acts 2:42, 46–47), later it was kept once a week on Sunday (Acts 20:7). The apostle did not say that they were to observe it as often as they met as a church body.

The Lord's Supper is not a sacrificial presentation to God; rather, it is a visible proclamation of the gospel message to men ("ye do show," *katangellete*). In the absence of Christ, all generations of believers are to observe the ordinance until He returns. When the kingdom is established, Christ Himself will officiate at His supper (cf. Matt. 26:29).

[21]The verb for "do" is a present imperative, literally meaning "Keep on doing." It shows that believers are to observe it over and over in their own lifetime (cf. Acts 2:42). The other two verbs are not found in the critical Greek text.

[22]There is a problem with the words "is broken." They are not found in the critical text; thus, the sense of substitution is left ("which is for you"). It is true that not one of his bones was broken (John 19:36), but his body was bruised with bones out of joint (Ps. 22:14). The concept of "broken" is not wrong if understood correctly.

C. The Chastisement of God (11:27–30)

Since the Lord's Supper was instituted by Christ and should be observed in remembrance of Him, it should be seen as a solemn occasion of worship. The Corinthians had violated its sanctity. Paul thus issued a warning, introduced by the resultant connective "wherefore" (*hōste*).

1. Its basis (11:27, 29b)

In this instance, chastisement is based upon an unworthy participation of the ordinance. The word "unworthily" (*anaxiōs*) is an adverb. The lack of worth does not refer to the person himself, but rather to the manner or attitude in which he eats. All are unworthy, including believers. Late in his life, Paul still saw himself as the chief of sinners (I Tim. 1:15). In himself, no one is worthy to approach God; but an unworthy person, saved by the grace of God, can partake in a worthy manner. However, the Corinthians were persistently[23] approaching the table unworthily.

Their sin was in "not discerning the Lord's body" (11:29b). The body could refer either to Christ's physical body (11:24) or to the mystical body of Christ, the true church (cf. 10:17; 12:13). Both, of course, were true. In their partiality and divisive spirit, they contradicted the truth of oneness in Christ. For this, they were "guilty" or liable (*enochos*). They were sinning in remembering the One who died to take away sins.

2. Its prevention (11:28)[24]

"Self-examination" by the believer should precede participation. He should put his life to the test by the objective standards of the Word of God. Does he love his spiritual brothers, all of them? Is he selfish? Christ taught that reconciliation between brethren should precede one's worship of God (cf. Matt. 5:23–26). After such examination and correction, then there should be a consistent participation in a worthy manner.

[23]The verbs for "eat" and "drink" are present subjunctives, indicating that their violations did not occur just once, but repeatedly.

[24]The word for "examine" (*dokimazetō*) is from the same root word as approved" (*dokimoi*, 11:19).

3. Its nature (11:29–30)

The general principle (11:29) is given before the specific application (11:30). Unworthy participation inevitably brings the chastisement of God. The word for "damnation" (*krima*) does not mean eternal punishment. The believer has forever been positionally delivered from hades and the lake of fire (cf. John 5:24; Rom. 8:1). Chastening is a sign of spiritual sonship and is designed as corrective discipline (cf. Heb. 12:3–11).

Specifically, some of the Corinthians had received degrees of chastisement, doubtless in direct proportion to the severity of their sins. "Many" (*polloi*) were physically weak, many others were sickly or diseased, and a sufficient number (*hikanoi*) had actually died. The word "sleep" (*koimōntai*) is used to depict the death of a believer in anticipation of the resurrection (John 11:11–14; Acts 7:60; I Cor. 15:51; I Thess. 4:13–18; II Peter 3:4).

D. The Judgment of the Believer (11:31–32)

Here, reasons are given for the necessity of self-judgment (11:31) and for the necessity of divine discipline (11:32).

1. The prevention of judgment (11:31)

Self-examination will prevent the judgment of God.[25] In this realm, believers are not to judge one another, but rather themselves. It should be a thorough, and not a superficial examination (note the prefix *dia* on *diekrinomen;* "we would judge"). It should also be a constant, daily examination (literally translated "If we keep on judging ourselves"). The believer should contrast what he is and what he should be, especially in his relationships with his fellow Christians.

2. The occurrence of judgment (11:32)

When a believer is being judged (*krinomenoi*), he is actually being chastened or disciplined as a father would correct his son for wrong behavior and would guide him toward proper goals. The word for "chastened" (*paideuometha*) is related to the word

---

[25]Paul stated this truth in a conditional, contrary-to-fact sentence. The fact of the matter is that the Corinthians were not judging themselves.

for "child" (*paidion*). God must judge sin wherever and in whomever He finds it. God must judge the believer for his post-conversion sin today because he has been delivered from the condemnation which awaits the unsaved at the great white throne and in the lake of fire (Rom. 8:1; cf. Rev. 20:11–15).[26] Thus, the judgment of God upon the believer for his sin is of a different character than that upon the unsaved for his sin.

E. The Counsel of Paul (11:33–34)

In spite of his criticism, Paul still addressed them as his brethren. He charged that when they came together in the church to eat the love feast and to observe the ordinance, they should wait for all of the members to arrive and that they should give time for self-examination and reconciliation.

Other counsel was given to the individual who looked upon the church meeting as an opportunity to fill his stomach. Paul charged him to eat his dinner at his home rather than in the church. This was necessary for both the individual and the church to avoid the judgment of God.

There were some other problems connected with the Lord's Supper ("the rest"; cf. 11:18), but Paul decided that he would deal with them personally when he revisited the church. Above all, Paul was concerned with orderly conduct (cf. 14:40).

QUESTIONS FOR DISCUSSION

1. Is the traditionally held concept of the headship of the man over the woman Scriptural? Defend your reply upon the basis of Scripture.

2. Is the evangelical feminist movement in harmony with the headship of man over the woman?

3. What contemporary cultural customs (dress, hair style, etc.) manifest the concept of subordination?

4. Do husbands and fathers perform their headship correctly? Why do they often fail in this area?

---

[26]The word for "condemnation" (Rom. 8:1, *katakrima*) is the same as that used in this verse (*katakrithōmen*).

5. How do the principles of this chapter apply to the single man? to the single woman?

6. Do modern Christians approach the ordinance of the Lord's Supper with reverence? If not, why is this so, and what can be done to correct this?

7. Should the ordinance be policed by the pastor, elders, and deacons? Should they forbid the elements to any?

8. Should the Lord's Supper be a service all by itself, or is it all right to observe it as a part of a regular service?

10

The Spiritual Gifts
I Corinthians 12 — 13

Paul again used the familiar connective phrase ("Now concerning," *peri de*; cf. 7:1, 25; 8:1) to show that he was moving to a new topic. Not only did the Corinthians have problems with the position of women and the observance of the Lord's Supper in their public worship services, but they also had questions about the exercise of spiritual gifts in their midst. The church was not "ignorant" of the existence of such gifts, but rather of their purpose and regulation (12:1; cf. 14:38; I Thess. 4:13).

The words "spiritual gifts" come from the Greek *tōn pneumatikōn*.[1] The words could refer either to the gifted believers[2] or to the gifts themselves. Actually, it is very difficult to distinguish between the gift and the person who has been gifted.[3]

Paul's treatment of this problem covers three chapters (chaps. 12–14). First he dealt with the relationship of the gifts to each other within the body of Christ (chap. 12); then he discussed their relationship to love and permanence (chap. 13); and

[1]Note that "gifts" is in italics in the English text.

[2]The Greek word grammatically can be either masculine in gender ("spiritual men") or neuter ("spiritual things or gifts"). There is a slight possibility that the phrase is specifically applied to the tongues-speakers (cf. 14:37). Their question, then, was about one group of gifted men. In his answer, Paul then related the gift of tongues to the other gifts (chap. 12), to love (chap. 13), and to prophecy (chap. 14).

[3]The spiritual man of this section is not the same as the one mentioned earlier (2:15; 3:2; Gal. 6:1). The Corinthians were spiritual in that the Spirit of God had gifted them, but they were carnal in their relationships to the Holy Spirit.

finally he concluded with a contrast between tongues and prophecy (chap. 14).

I. GIFTS AND THE BODY OF CHRIST (12:1–31)

The normal word for gifts is *charismatōn* (12:4),[4] literally meaning "grace gifts." Thus, a spiritual gift is an ability given to the Christian out of the grace of God through the Holy Spirit and controlled by the Spirit in Christian service and growth.[5]

A. Influence of the Supernatural (12:2–3)

1. Demons over pagans (12:2)

Paul reminded them that in their pagan past they had been dominated by Satan and by demons (cf. 10:19-20). The verb "carried away" (*apagomenoi*) was used of a prisoner being led away (Mark 14:44; 15:16) and here it indicates that they had been controlled by outside forces. That influence did not come from the idols themselves because idols were dumb (cf. Ps. 95:5–7; Hab. 2:18–19). Unconsciously, they were deceived by the world of evil spirits. The pagan priests, when they spoke ecstatic words in their trances, also were under the influence of demons.

2. Demons over professing Christians (12:3a)

He informed them that no person "speaking" under the influence of the Holy Spirit would proclaim a heretical doctrine about Jesus Christ.[6] Any person who would do so would either have to be unsaved or be under the influence of demons.[7] The phrase "speaking by [literally, "in"] the Spirit of God" could refer either to a supernaturally given prophetic announcement (cf.

---

[4]The contemporary charismatic movement takes its name from this word.

[5]For a more detailed discussion of the gifts, see John F. Walvoord, *The Holy Spirit,* pp. 168–188. For their relationship to the modern charismatic movement, see Robert Gromacki, *The Modern Tongues Movement.*

[6]Approximately one-fourth of worldwide Pentecostalism denies the orthodox doctrine of the trinity. Known as the "Jesus Only" group, they claim that there is only one person within the divine Essence or Being.

[7]Some respected evangelicals have reported to me experiences of believers speaking blasphemies under the influence of demons.

The Sacred Spring, in Corinth. Ruins of the temple of Apollo are visible in the background, upper right.

Matt. 22:43; Acts 28:25; II Peter 1:21) or to a tongues-utterance
(cf. II Thess. 2:2), or to both. The word "accursed" (*anathema*; cf.
Gal. 1:8–9) is very similar to the Greek word for "offering"
(*anathēma*, translated as "gift" in Luke 21:5). Also, notice this
closeness of sounds in this verse: "If any man love not the Lord
Jesus Christ, let him be Anathema Maran-atha" (16:22). Thus, it
could have been that a person tried to simulate a real tongues-
utterance with faulty pronunciation, resulting in a heretical
declaration.

3. The Holy Spirit over real Christians (12:3b)

Only a person controlled by the Holy Spirit can properly
proclaim the deity of Jesus Christ (12:3b). Naturally, anyone can
utter the words without meaning or commitment (cf. Matt.
7:21–23).

B. Source of Gifts (12:4–6)

Christians should know that the genuine source of spiritual
gifts is the one and only triune God. Note the contrast between
the threefold use of "diversities" (*diaireseis*)[8] and the threefold
use of "same" in this passage. The word "diversities" implies
division, distribution, allotment, or apportionment. It suggests
that all believers receive at least one gift and that no believer
receives all of the gifts.

The source of the different "gifts" (*charismatōn*) is "the same
Spirit" (12:4); the source of the different "administrations"
(*diakoniōn*; "ministries" and "deacons" are based upon this word)
is "the same Lord," namely, Jesus Christ (cf. 3:5); and the source
of the different "operations" (*energēmatōn*; "energies" is a transliteration) is "the same God" and Father who works (*energōn*; cf.
Phil. 2:13) or energizes "all [things] in all [men]." Since there is
no competition among the persons of the divine Oneness in the
giving of the gifts,[9] there should be no jealousy between gifted
believers in the one body of Christ. Complementary harmony of

[8]This Greek word is translated both as "diversities" and "differences" in this
passage.

[9]Note the order of mention: Spirit, Christ, Father. Since there is an equality of
persons within the divine Essence, the order can vary.

purpose and cooperation should prevail. Unity and diversity are not rivals, but partners in God's redemptive program (cf. Eph. 4:3–11).

C. List of Gifts (12:7–11)

In the divine economy, the Holy Spirit gives the abilities, the Son assigns the gifted believer a definite ministry, and the Father controls the entire operation. Thus, in this section, Paul pointed out the prominent part that the Spirit of God plays in the distribution of the various gifts.

1. The Spirit gives gifts to every believer (12:7)

No believer is excluded: no believer is without a supernaturally given ability to perform a spiritual service for God. Four features are pointed out. First, it is a manifestation of the Spirit. Just as one life principle within the human body causes the physical eye to see and the ear organ to hear, so each gift manifests the presence of both eternal life and the Spirit in the person's life. Second, it is a gift. It cannot be bought or earned. Third, it is given to each Christian (the phrase "to everyman" [*hekastōi*] actually occurs in the emphatic first position of the verse). Fourth, it is given for the purpose of the common good, the "profit" of both the person and the body.

2. The Spirit gives different gifts to different believers (12:8–10)

Nine specific gifts are mentioned here, but there are others (cf. 12:28–30; Rom. 12:3–8; Eph. 4:7–11). Here the gifts are stressed, but the other lists emphasize both the gift and the office of the gifted man (12:28–30), the gift and its duty (Rom. 12:3–8), and the office of the gifted man (Eph. 4:7–11). The gifts fall into three categories: the first consisting of wisdom and knowledge; the second of faith, healings, miracles, prophecy, and discerning of spirits; and the third of tongues and interpretation.[10]

What were the purposes or the meanings of the gifts?[11]

[10]This cannot be detected from the English text, but the Greek definitely shows the threefold break in the words translated as "one" and "another." Note the use of *hōi* for wisdom; *heterōi* for faith; and *heterōi* for tongues. All the others have *allōi*.

[11]It is difficult to be dogmatic because of the lack of adequate information.

The word of wisdom referred to the revelation of the mind of God in doctrinal, redemptive areas (cf. 2:6–7). This was not learned or acquired wisdom, but divinely imparted. Paul both received and communicated this wisdom (II Peter 3:15).

The word of knowledge could have referred to the revelation of exhortations in the practical areas of life (cf. Eph. 4–6).

All Christians are justified by faith and should walk by faith (Heb. 11), but the gift of "faith" is a special faith to attempt great tasks for God (cf. 13:2). It seems to be connected with outward demonstrations of God's power (12:9–10; cf. 13:2).

The gift of interpretation was the translation of the tongues-to heal the sick of various diseases (e.g., palsy, leprosy, blindness).

The working of miracles involved power over nature (cf. Acts 5:1–10; 13:11; Gal. 3:5; Heb. 2:4). These miracles were designed to authenticate divine spokesmen (cf. II Cor. 12:12).

The gift of prophecy involved both foretelling and forth-telling, the communication of a message direct from God to men (cf. 14:3). The foundation of the church was laid by the apostles and the prophets (Eph. 2:20; cf. Acts 11:28; 19:6; 21:11).

The gift of discerning of spirits (cf. I John 4:1) was the ability to "discern the true from the false sources of supernatural revelation given in oral form."[12]

The gift of tongues was the Spirit-given ability to speak in known, foreign languages (unknown and unlearned by the speaker).[13] The content involved the revelation of divine mysteries (cf. 14:2) marked by magnifying God.

The gift of interpretation was the translation of the tongues-utterance into the common language by one who did not know the language of the tongues-speaker.

3. The Spirit decides which gift to give (12:11)

He "works" (energei), "divides" (diairoun; verbal form of "diversities"), and "wills" (bouletai). His choices are sovereign. There is no indication that the prayers of believers affect His decisions.

---

[12]John F. Walvoord, Holy Spirit, p. 188.

[13]There is much disagreement here. Both contemporary glossolalists and non-tongues-speaking commentators believe that these were utterances in languages totally unknown to any human culture.

D. Oneness of the Body (12:12–13)

1. One body (12:12)

Paul wanted the Corinthians to recognize their spiritual oneness within the body of Christ. To do so, he showed a similarity between the human body and the true church. The human body has many parts or members, but it is still one body (12:12a). This truth was stated in two ways: one body has many members and many members make one body. The analogy is clear: "so also is Christ" (12:12b). The equation of Christ with His mystical body, the church, can be seen here. Christ said to Saul who had devastated the church: "Why persecutest thou me?" (Acts 9:4; cf. Eph. 5:23; Col. 1:18). There is one church, not many churches (Matt. 16:18; Eph. 1:22–23; 4:4), and all believers, regardless of their race, sex, social status, or denominational affiliation, belong to that one church.

2. One baptism (12:13a)

The human body is conceived and born with its many members intact, but believing sinners become members of the true church through the baptism in the Holy Spirit (12:13a). All believers possess equally the seven unities: One body, one spirit, one hope, one Lord, one faith, one baptism, one God and Father (Eph. 4:4–6). This baptism cannot refer to water baptism nor its mode because all believers have not been water baptized nor have they all been immersed or sprinkled. Christ predicted that He would build His church (Matt. 16:18 — still future during his earthly ministry) which was later designated as His body (Eph. 1:22–23). A person becomes a member of that body by the baptism in (Greek *en*; "in" better than "by") the Holy Spirit, predicted by Christ (Acts 1:5) and accomplished the first time on the day of Pentecost (Acts 2:2).[14] The baptism in the Spirit, therefore, is not a postconversion experience to be sought by all and to be achieved by some. There is no command in Scripture to be baptized in the Spirit. *All* believers ("we all" included both the spiritual Paul and the carnal Corinthians) were baptized at the time of their conversion.

---

[14]The Spirit "filled all the house where they were sitting" (Acts 2:2). They were literally in the Spirit, immersed or baptized in Him.

3. One drink (12:13b)

In addition, all believers have received the indwelling presence of the Spirit ("have been all made to drink"; cf. John 7:38–39). Not only are they in the Spirit, but the Spirit is in them. There is no believer who does not have the Holy Spirit within him (cf. Rom. 8:9).

E. Diversity of Members (12:14–18)

In this section, Paul wanted the Christians to recognize their functional diversity within the one body of Christ. Four principles are stated.

1. The body performs many functions (12:14)

One member does not constitute a body. An arm, by itself, is not a body. Neither are members, dissected from each other, a body. To be a body, all the members must function and be organically related to each other. Thus, all Christians should not expect to have the same gift (e.g., tongues, miracles, or teaching).

2. Each function is important (12:15–16)

No member should belittle his importance just because he cannot do the functions of other members. Neither can a foot be a hand nor an ear an eye. This inability does not remove its membership or functional necessity within the body. Thus, a member should not covet the function of another.

3. Each function must be performed (12:17)

If all members performed only one function, then other necessary functions would go undone. A body consisting of only an eye or an ear would be a monstrosity.

4. God assigns each function (12:18)

God decides what each member will be, when he will function, and where. God framed the human body by giving it two eyes in the front of the head and two ears on each respective side. So it is with the true church. God sovereignly gifts believers and assigns them special functions. They are not given these responsibilities because they are better than others, but because God was "pleased" (*ēthelēsen,* normally translated as "willed") to do it. The giving of the gifts apparently occurs at the moment of salvation when the person is placed within the body of Christ by the baptism in the Holy Spirit.

F. Mutual Need of Members (12:19–21)

Paul repeated his basic premise: "one body" with "many members." A body, to be a body, must have many members (12:19). The members, to be members, must be organically related to the other members within one body (12:20). A Christian is wrong in feeling that he has "no need" of the ministries of other believers (12:21). The eye needs the hand and the head can do nothing without the feet. Thus, a Christian should not think that he is independent, self-sufficient, or better than others.

G. Importance of All Members (12:22–26)

Up to this point, Paul had talked about the conspicious members of the human body for his illustrations of spiritual ministries: foot, hand, ear, eye, and nose. To press his analogy, Paul now introduced those members which are not readily observed. In so doing, he set forth three major principles.

1. Importance is not based upon appearance (12:22–23)

The importance and honor of individual members should not be based upon outward appearance, a cursory observation, or a superficial evaluation of their contributions to the body. What man calls "feeble" is really necessary. The word translated "feeble" is *asthenestera,* which conveys the idea of weakness (same root word as for "weak" brother in 8:10). To man, some believers "seem to be" weak in that they do not seem to bring strength or honor to the body; but to God (note "much more") they are absolutely necessary. The little toe may seem to be insignificant, but try to walk or run without one. The liver and kidneys are not as impressive as brown eyes or bulging biceps, but try to live without them!

In fact, man "bestows" (*peritithemen;* literally, "places around") upon those parts of his body, which he deems to be unattractive, expensive clothing (12:23). Thus, he covers up his ugly feet with stylish shoes and his poor physique with tailored suits. In so doing, he draws attention away from his innately attractive parts (eyes, nose) to his "uncomely parts" which are now fashionably attired.

2. Importance is equally distributed (12:24–25)

Through clothing and lack of clothing, a balance of honor and recognition is achieved (12:24b). The eyes, nose, mouth, or teeth do not need to be covered since they have the quality of beauty and attraction within themselves. God made or "tempered" (synekerasen; literally, "to mix together"; cf. Heb. 4:2) the body in this way so that all members would receive equality of recognition and honor (12:24b).

Two reasons are given for this divine design: one negative and one positive (12:25). First, to prevent schism (cf. 1:10), conflict of interest, or a superiority-inferiority complex, no member of the body (gifted believer) should be praised or neglected at the expense of the others. Second, to promote mutual care or concern for each other, believers should not compete against another, but should love and minister to each other (cf. Gal. 6:1–5).

3. Importance belongs to the entire body (12:26)

All members (the total body) suffer when one member becomes injured or diseased (12:26a). A broken wrist bone or a lung full of cancer affects the entire person, not just that one part of the body. All members rejoice when one member is isolated for recognition (12:26b). A crown is given to the person for having the most beautiful eyes. In the Olympics, the gold medal is placed around the neck of the fastest athlete, not over his feet.

H. Sovereignty over the Members (12:27–30)

1. God chose the members (12:27)

After the fitting analogy (12:14–26), Paul affirmed: "Now ye are the body of Christ, and members in particular" (12:27). Corporately, all of the Corinthian believers comprised the manifestation of the universal body of Christ in that geographic region. They were not *the* one and only body in the entire world (note that "the" does not occur in the Greek). This indicates that all genuine believers who were baptized in the Spirit into the universal body also affiliated themselves with the local church. There were no believers outside of the fellowship of the local assembly. Individually, each Corinthian believer was a member and therefore should function with others even as the parts of the human body complement each other.

2. God established the order of the members (12:28)

Note the sequence of the words: "first . . . secondarily . . . thirdly . . . after that . . . then." Although not all of the nine previously mentioned gifts are named,[15] a clear distinction between the gift of apostleship, which Paul possessed, and the gift of tongues, which they exalted, can be seen. His was first, and theirs was last. The verb "hath set" (*etheto*) indicates that God made the appointments in His own interest; thus men do not choose their own gifts. The order also goes from persons (including both office and gift) to the gifts themselves.

3. God determined the number of members (12:29–30)

In a series of seven questions, all demanding the negative answer,[16] Paul forcefully argued that all believers could not be apostles nor speak in tongues. Earlier, he had stated that the entire body could not be reduced to one member. The body has two eyes, two ears, ten fingers, and one heart. Apparently, the quantity of gifted men is also so apportioned. Only fifteen were designated as apostles (the twelve, Paul, James, and Barnabas).

Also, the principle of temporary gifts can be seen in that apostles functioned only in the first century in that they had to be commissioned directly by the resurrected Christ (cf. 9:1–6; Gal. 1:1). The gift expired when the person who had the gift died. Its purpose for existence had ended, according to the divine will.

---

[15] In fact, new gifts are inserted into the discussion: apostles, teachers, helps, and governments.

[16] Each question uses the negative *mē*.

II. GIFTS AND LOVE (12:31—13:13)

God also established that the *way* in which believers perform their tasks is more important than *what* they do (12:31). Paul wanted the Corinthians to go beyond their present pursuit. To the apostle, the development of the character of the person was superior to the exercise of the gift. His contrasts (chap. 13) are clear: gifts without love vs. gifts with love, and the permanence of love vs. the temporal nature of the gifts. There is no indication that Paul is asking them to choose between a quest for gifts and that of love.

The verb "covet" can be taken in two different ways. It may mean that Paul wanted them to desire the manifestation of those gifts which would contribute to the greatest harmony and edification of the church (gifts listed first, cf. 12:28) or it may mean that Paul was charging them with the sin of jealousy in coveting the conspicuous, showy gifts for their own self-exaltation. This verb (*zēloute*) is based upon the noun translated "emulations" (*zēlos*, Gal. 5:20), one of the works of the sinful flesh. The latter seems to be more appropriate in this context.

A. Necessity of Love (13:1–3)

The Greeks elevated what a man knew (his intellect), the Romans worshiped what a man could do (his power), but Paul stressed what a man is (his character). The pinnacle of spiritual development is to love[17] God with the total being and to love one's neighbor as himself. In the exercise of spiritual gifts, this is no less important. The apostle cited three hypothetical[18] illustrations to demonstrate the necessity of love in Christian service.

1. In speaking (13:1)

The "sounding brass" was a noisy gong, made of brass (alloy of copper and tin) rather than a poorly played trumpet. The "tinkling cymbal" gave a clashing, inarticulated (*alalazon*) sound.

[17]The normal and best translation for *agapē* is "love" rather than "charity" in these verses.

[18]The word "though" is a translation of the conditional *ean* used with the subjunctive verbal mood.

A large section of the ancient Roman aqueduct that brought water to Pisidian Antioch. Such constructions typify the power and influence of the Romans.

Although tongues[19] was the least gift, it was the center of controversy, and so Paul used it as his first example.

2. In knowing (13:2)

The gifts of prophecy, wisdom, knowledge, and faith without love reveal the selfishness and unimportance of a person's character before God (13:2). Notice the threefold use of "all" — with "mysteries," "knowledge," and "faith." A full head with an empty heart is worth nothing.

3. In giving (13:3)

Compassion and martyrdom, although admired by all, will receive no heavenly reward if done apart from genuine love for God and man. The conclusion is evident: If love is so necessary, then it is imperative that a believer produce the fruit of the Spirit (Gal. 5:22–23) in the midst of his service.

---

[19]The "tongues of men" show that glossolalia was in foreign languages and dialects of various human cultures. The "tongues of angels" was not an unknown, ecstatic utterance; rather, angels and men conversed together in common languages known to men.

B. Nature of Love (13:4–7)

Sixteen properties of love are enumerated here. Thus, a Christian has not been perfected in love unless all sixteen characteristics are seen in his life simultaneously. He cannot claim the possession of love if only one or a few of them can be superficially seen in his behavior.

1. In relationship to others (13:4a)

To "suffer long" is to be patient with *people* who aggravate you, rather than with impersonal circumstances (e.g., a long red light). To be "kind" is to do good to those who are irritating you. To "envy not"[20] is to be pleased with the success of others who advance, perhaps even at your expense.

2. In relationship to self (13:4b–5a)

To be void of "vaunting" is not to brag about one's abilities or achievements. To be "puffed up" is to be proud over one's position and to see oneself as superior to others (cf 8:1). To "behave unseemly" is to act boorishly, not as a gentleman — respecting the needs of others. To seek "one's own" profit, pleasure, or edification as a goal in itself is selfish.

3. In relationship to sin (13:5b–6)

To be "provoked"[21] is to be driven to wrathful anger caused by offense. A Puritan once wrote: "I am determined so to be angry as not to sin; therefore to be angry with nothing but sin" (cf. Eph. 4:26–27). To "think no evil" is to see the best in others and to plot no harm against them. Love will "not rejoice" in the sins or misfortunes of others. Love will "rejoice in the truth" by speaking it (Eph. 4:15) and by walking in it (II John 4).

4. In relationship to circumstances (13:7)

Love "bears all things" in that it conceals what is displeasing in others (cf. James 5:20; I Peter 4:8). It believes all things in that it is not suspicious of the deeds and motivations of others. It

[20]This verb (*zēloi*) is the same as "covet" (12:31). Love does not covet gifts for its own satisfaction.

[21]The adverb "easily" does not appear in the Greek text.

hopes all things by anticipating the spiritual good that will result from wrongdoing (cf. Rom. 8:28). It endures all things in that it willingly puts up with awkward circumstances caused by unloving brethren.

5. In relationship to everything (13:8a)

In his summary statement, Paul claimed that love will never fail. In all circumstances and human relationships, when in doubt: "Love!" It is never wrong to love. Love will always triumph. That conclusion also served as a fitting transition into the next section.

C. Permanence of Love (13:8–13)

Solomon wrote: "Many waters cannot quench love, neither can the floods drown it" (Song of Sol. 5:7). To contrast the permanence of love with the transitory character of the gifts, Paul made six observations.

1. Gifts are temporary (13:8)

The gift of prophecy will "fail," or be rendered null and void (*katargēthēsontai*); the gift of tongues will cease to function (*pausontai*); and the gift of revealed knowledge will likewise be rendered void or "vanish away" (*katargēthēsetai*). Paul did not refer to the content of the revealed prophecy, glossolalia, or knowledge because God's revealed Word, whether written or spoken, will last forever. The truth of those utterances will be experienced in the eternal state by all believers. The appointment of gifts, however, will end. Both verbs used for prophecy and knowledge are identical and indicate that their purpose will be rendered useless by the influence of something outside of themselves. However, the verb for *tongues* reveals that its purpose will cease on its own even before the coming of that which will render the other two unnecessary.

2. Gifts are partial (13:9)

Just as one member does not comprise the entire body nor does it perform the functions of all of the other members, so those gifted with either prophecy or knowledge only communicate that which God has revealed to them. God has never revealed to one man all of the divine purpose; rather, He has progressively revealed His will through past generations by His selected spokesmen (cf. Heb. 1:1-2). The Bible was not written by one man, but by approximately forty over a span of sixteen hundred years.

3. Gifts will end (13:10)

The partial gifts will be rendered inoperative at the coming of "that which is perfect" (13:10). In this context, the partial gifts are prophecy and knowledge; it was not said of tongues that it was partial. The verb "shall be done away" is just another translation of the same verb (katargēthēsetai) translated earlier as "shall fail" and "shall vanish away" (13:8).

The main problem here is in the meaning of the phrase "that which is perfect" (to teleion). Two major views have emerged. First, the adherents of Pentecostalism and many noncharismatic evangelicals believe that it refers to the coming of Christ and its attendant events; thus, according to them, the spiritual gifts were all designed to be permanent. The absence of such gifts from the life of the church in past generations is attributed to a lack of teaching and faith.

The second view claims that the phrase refers to the completion of divine revelation, both written and oral, accomplished with the writing of the last book of the Bible (Revelation) by the last living apostle (John). This means that these gifts of revelation and authentication were temporary, designed for the first century only. In this view, the gift of tongues ended even before A.D. 95, probably with the destruction of Jerusalem and the dispersion of the Jews (A.D. 70; cf. 14:21-22). Again, dogmatism is not possible, but a careful study of all of the the arguments, pro and con, seems to favor the second view.[22]

4. Gifts are infantile (13:11)

The partial gifts, like infancy, are to be superceded by adulthood (13:11). Note the triple analogy of infancy to the gifts: "spoke as a child" (tongues; cf. 14:18-20); "understood as a child" (knowledge); and "thought as a child" (wisdom and

---

[22]See the author's discussion in The Modern Tongues Movement, pp. 122-129.

prophecy). Just as Paul "put away" (*katērgēka;* same verb as "fail," "vanish," and "done away") the expressions of his physical infancy when he became an adult, so the church was to render null and void those gifts which were needed only during its period of infancy. The church received adulthood when its spiritual nurses, the apostles, were removed (Eph. 4:1–16; note the expressions "no more children," "grown up," and "perfect man" [same word — *teleion*]; cf. I Thess 2:6–7).

5. Knowledge is progressive (13:12)

Both partial and mature knowledge will become full knowledge in the presence of Christ. The "glass" was really a mirror, made of polished metal. At best, it gave a blurry, distorted image. By looking into the mirror of the written Word of God, a believer could grasp some understanding of what he is and what he will be before God, but that knowledge cannot compare with that which he will have when he sees the Savior.

6. Love is eternal (13:13)

Love abides throughout time and eternity. Even the great qualities of faith and hope are limited to time; they are likewise temporal because one day faith will become sight and hope will become reality. But, love lasts forever. The familiar triad of faith, hope, and love can be seen in many other passages (Rom. 5:2–5; Gal. 5:5; Col. 1:4; I Thess. 1:3; 5:8; Heb. 6:10–12; I Peter 1:21–22).

QUESTIONS FOR DISCUSSION

1. If demons can attack the minds of Christians, can they also cause believers to speak passively in unknown sounds? If so, what can be done to correct this?

2. Why is there so much emphasis on the spiritual gifts today?

3. Can a person have a spiritual gift without knowing it? Can it be developed? Can it be lost?

4. How can all members of a local church make a contribution to the life of the assembly? What programs help or hinder this type of participation?

5. If someone claims to have the gift of apostleship or tongues, how can this assertion be proved or disproved?

6. Do denominations and independent churches destroy the unity of the true church? Can there be cooperation when there are distinct differences of doctrine?

7. Is revelation still taking place today? What about visions, dreams, tongues-utterances?

Contrast Between
Prophecy and Tongues
I Corinthians 14

An early church father, Chrysostom, made this comment: "This whole passage is very obscure; but the obscurity arises from our ignorance of the facts described, which, though familiar to those to whom the apostle wrote, have ceased to occur."[1] In his opinion, the gift of tongues was temporary, limited to the apostolic era. Although much desirable information about the gifts is lacking, enough is given in this chapter to draw a firm contrast between prophecy and tongues. There is no doubt that Paul expressed a preference for prophecy. He began and ended this section with commands to desire it (14:1; cf. 14:39). In between, the arguments for the superiority of prophecy are clear and decisive. His approach to the contrast can be seen in four divisions, marked off by the triple use of the vocative "Brethren" (14:6, 20, 26).

I. IN ESSENCE (14:1–5)

The first major contrast is based upon the very nature of the two gifts: what they are in themselves. We will discuss their definitions, their relationships to God and to men, and their respective value for spiritual edification.

A. Paul's Preference (14:1)

The opening verse of this chapter resumes Paul's earlier directive (cf. 12:31). After he described the more excellent way of

---

[1] Cited by Charles Hodge, *Commentary on the First Epistle to the Corinthians*, pp. 277–78.

love, the apostle charged: "Follow after [love]." The verb (*diōkete*) means to pursue diligently with the anticipation of seizing the goal (cf. Phil. 3:12, 14). The life of love was to be their first priority. At the same time, they were to desire the gifts. Earlier, Paul had mentioned "the best gifts" (12:31); now, he pointed out the superiority of prophecy over tongues. According to Morris, prophecy was "not the delivery of a carefully prepared sermon, but the uttering of words directly inspired of God."[2] Thus, "follow" is stronger than "desire," and among the gifts prophecy was better than tongues.

B. Purposes (14:2–3)

The reason for desiring prophecy over tongues is seen in the explanatory "for."

1. Purpose of tongues (14:2)

First, the tongues-speaker does not speak to men or for men.[3] Second, he rather speaks to God. In this sense, it involved praise, probably through simple declaration, praying, and singing (cf. 14:14–16; Acts 2:11; 10:46). Third, no one present understands the tongues-speaker. If the gift of tongues involved speaking in foreign languages never learned by the speaker, then no person in attendance at the meeting could understand in his native tongue.[4] The word "unknown" appears in italics (14:2, 4, 15, 19, 27) and is not in the Greek text. Those who claim that tongues was in unintelligible ecstatic speech believe that no one could understand for that very reason.[5] Fourth, he speaks in the spirit (*pneumati*). Although this could refer to the Holy Spirit,[6] it probably means the human spirit (cf. "spirit" is

[2]Leon Morris, *The First Epistle of Paul to the Corinthians*, p. 190.

[3]The dative case (*anthrōpois*) can be translated and interpreted either way.

[4]These also believe that tongues was always in foreign languages. Cf. Hodge, *Corinthians*, pp. 277–78, and S. Lewis Johnson, "The First Epistle to the Corinthians" *The Wycliffe Bible Commentary*, p. 1253.

[5]See James Boyer, *For a World Like Ours*, p. 131; and F. W. Grosheide, *Commentary on the First Epistle to the Corinthians*, p. 318.

[6]Held by Hodge, *Corinthians*, p. 279.

used in this way elsewhere — 14:14, 32).[7] Fifth, he speaks "mysteries." A mystery was a divine truth, unknown in the past, but revealed by God in the present. Thus, tongues was a revelatory, authenticating ability.

2. Purpose of prophecy (14:3)

First, one who prophesies speaks directly to men in their common language. Second, he speaks words of edification. Third, he speaks words of "exhortation" (*paraklēsin*). This is designed to strengthen and to encourage (cf. I Thess. 3:2). Fourth, he speaks words of comfort to those who are depressed (cf. John 11:19, 31; Phil. 2:1; I Thess. 2:12). The prophet thus has a threefold goal in his preaching: Build up, stir up, and cheer up.

C. Edification (14:4–5)

1. Recipients of edification (14:4)

The tongues-speaker simply edified himself. The manner in which this was accomplished is not stated. His profit may have come through his awareness that he was an instrument of praise even though he did not know what was being said. In any case, self-edification was contrary to the spirit of love (cf. 13:5; "seeks not her own") and to the relationship of the members to each other. Self-edification, though, is a worthy fringe benefit of ministering to others.

Contrariwise, the prophet exercised his gift for the edification of the entire church. This corresponded to the real purpose behind gifts (cf. 12:7, 25; 14:12, 26). Although the tongues-speaker had the right or liberty to exercise his gift, it was wrong to do so without love and without interpretation.

2. Superiority in edification (14:5)

The apostle then clearly declared that the prophet was "greater" (*meizōn*; same word as "best," 12:31) than the tongues-speaker. This comparison was just between the two gifts and their direct value for edification. He then noted that, if the tongues-speaker also had the gift of interpretation, and used it,

[7]Held by Morris, *Corinthians*, p. 191.

he was equal to the prophet because the church would receive equal edification.

Paul's wish ("I would that ye all spake with tongues") must be seen as his desire for them to receive self-edification in their ministry to others. The same word (*thelō*) is used of his wish for men and women to remain single (7:7), but he knew that marriage was inevitable for the majority. So also God wishes all men to be saved, but all men will not be converted (cf. I Tim. 2:4). Thus, Paul knew that all would never speak in tongues because that was contrary to the divine program (cf. 12:7, 11, 18, 30).

II. IN UNDERSTANDING (14:6–20)

Do you understand what you are doing? Do others understand what you are doing? Once Paul had defined the essence of tongues-speaking, he wanted his readers to answer those questions. He arrested their attention by the connective "Now," by the direct address "Brethren," and by the insertion of himself as an example ("if I come . . . what shall I profit you").

A. Communication (14:6–11)

Paul used four analogies to show that understanding must result from all forms of communication.

1. In Paul's ministry (14:6)

Later, Paul announced that he intended a return visit to Corinth (16:3–7). He now theorized that if he came into their midst with only uninterpreted tongues-utterances they would receive no spiritual profit. Rather, they could receive immense spiritual edification if he ministered in at least one of four different ways. Revelation involved the imparting of truth previously unknown (perhaps the word of wisdom). The word of knowledge was the unfolding of the divine will for practical decisions. The gift of prophecy involved both foretelling and forthtelling (cf. 14:3). "Doctrine" (*didachēi* is based upon the word for "teacher") related an explanation of those divine truths necessary for true orthodoxy.

2. In music (14:7)

The "pipe" was a flute, a representative of all wind instruments; the "harp" (*kithara* is the basis of the English "guitar") is a symbol of all stringed instruments. Genuine music is not unintelligible noise. To be played properly and to be appreciated and understood, it must envelop a series of notes in harmony. They must make musical sense.

3. In military warfare (14:8)

Trumpets were used for different purposes: to wake up the sleeping army, to prepare for battle, to retreat, to rest, and to stand for drill (14:8). The mere blowing of the trumpet was not sufficient. There had to be distinctions in the pitch of the sound, in the length of the blast, and in the repetition of the call, or else there would be utter confusion in the camp (cf. 14:33, 40).

4. In daily conversation (14:9–11)

The analogy is clear from the illustrations drawn from the worlds of music and war ("so likewise ye"). The word "ye" (*humeis*) is very emphatic. To transmit truth orally, one must use words whose meanings are known; words that are grammatically related to each other; and words that are articulated, not mumbled or slurred.[8] If this does not take place, then a speaker is only mouthing meaningless sound waves into the air. Speech is designed to communicate thoughts, not merely to make noise with the vocal cords.

Paul reinforced his argument by an appeal to the spoken languages of the world's population (14:10). All languages, whether written or spoken by either civilized or uncivilized peoples, have vocabulary meanings, verbal syntax, and in some cases tonal distinctions.[9] Bible translators in primitive areas have often been amazed at the sophisticated language structure of natives who could not read or write. A play on words is found in

[8]This can apply to the lack of understanding by the suburbanite of ghetto slang, by adults of youth talk, and by the Catholic laity of a Latin mass.

[9]Linguists have taped the utterances of tongues-speakers and have declared them to be nonlanguages according to the necessary characteristics inherent in known languages and dialects.

this verse: A "voice" (*phōnē*) is not a "nonvoice" (*aphōnon* translated as "without signification"). To Paul, there was no difference between real dumbness and unintelligible utterances; in neither is there communication of ideas for profit.

The apostle then lengthened his analogy to two civilized people who spoke and understood two different languages (14:11).[10] To each other, they were barbarians. In that day, a barbarian was regarded as one ignorant of culture and language, living outside of the civilized Roman Empire. To Paul, communication was intrinsic to the divine purpose; it was "the name of the game."

B. Prayer (14:12–17)

1. Prayer for interpretation (14:12–13)

Paul wanted the Corinthians to apply the logic of the analogies to their spiritual interests ("even so ye"). He also wanted them to transfer their zeal for tongues to that of church edification (14:12). He did not praise or condemn them for being "gift zealots"; rather, he wanted them to redirect that enthusiasm for the edification of others through proper communication. The words "spiritual gifts" are really a translation of *pneumatōn*, normally translated "spirits." They apparently coveted people whose human spirits were the channels of the spectacular gifts, especially that of tongues (cf. 14:2, 14, 32; I John 4:1).

At Corinth, there apparently was an abundance of tongues-speakers, but few, if any, interpreters (14:13). In the services, three could speak in tongues, and that in turn ("by course") but only one could interpret (cf. 14:27). There was the distinct possibility that no interpreter would even be present at the meeting (14:28). Because profit through understanding was Paul's main thrust, he advised the tongues-speaker to pray for the gift of interpretation. He was not to pray for the interpretation after he had spoken in tongues; rather, in advance of the meeting, he was to seek the ability of interpretation so that when the service occurred, the tongues-utterances could be translated for the

[10]The author experienced this in Brazil with saved and unsaved Brazilians who could only speak and read Portuguese. An interpreter was absolutely necessary.

171

edification of the church (cf. 14:5). The presence of the interpreter in the meeting had to be known in advance or else those who had the gift of tongues were to remain silent (14:28). If one could pray and receive the interpretation after speaking in tongues, then there would always be a potential interpreter present and there would be no rationale to the apostolic directive.

2. Prayer for understanding (14:14–17)

Three specific examples are cited to show the necessity of spiritual understanding: praying, singing, and blessing or giving thanks (14:14–17). Tongues-speaking could be prayer by the human spirit (note "*my* spirit");[11] but even then, the understanding (*nous*; literally, the "mind") was not involved. The person praying in tongues did not know what he was saying; therefore, there was no spiritual development within him. To Paul, there was only one logical conclusion ("What is it then?"). Prayer, to be profitable, must involve both the human spirit and the human understanding (14:15a). Prayer in a common language would achieve this. Proponents of the charismatic movement would argue that one could pray in tongues and then pray with the intellect (*via* interpretation) or else that he could pray devotionally in tongues in private and publicly in a common language. However, the passage seems to indicate one prayer employing both the spirit and the understanding, or intellect (14:15a). Uninterpreted tongues-praying is not profitable either in private or in public.

Tongues-speaking could also include singing, but again Paul argued that it must involve both the spirit and the understanding, or mind (14:15b), to accomplish spiritual profit in the lives of both the speaker and the listener (14:15). To "sing" (*psallō*) generally means to sing to the accompaniment of musical instruments (cf. Eph. 5:19).

Tongues-speaking could also include the giving of a "blessing" (*eulogeō*) or the "giving of thanks" to God (*eucharisteō*). But it must be understood in order to achieve three goals: to enlist the participation of others, to give understanding, and to promote

[11]Nowhere is the Holy Spirit called "my spirit."

edification (14:16–17). The recitation of the "Amen" manifested the response of the congregation to public prayer (cf. I Chron. 16:36; Neh. 8:6; Ps. 106:48). The "unlearned" (*idiōtou*) may refer either to sympathetic Gentile inquirers in attendance at the church meeting or to new Christians who were totally unfamiliar with the manifestation of the spectacular gifts.

C. Public Teaching (14:18–20)

1. The source of teaching (14:18–19)

Any gift that God has given must be received with thanksgiving (14:18). Paul spoke in tongues, and he was grateful. The phrase "more than ye all" may mean that the gift had a superior manifestation in his life than it did in the lives of the Corinthians. Each Corinthian tongues-speaker apparently spoke in this one language (note use of singular, 14:2, 4, 13), but Paul could speak in many languages when he used the gift (note use of plural, 14:6, 18; cf. Acts 2:8-11). It does not mean that Paul spoke more often in tongues than they did.

The apostle then clearly stated that *in the church* (the meeting of believers for worship and instruction) he would rather speak five words which could be understood by his listeners than innumerable words[12] in uninterpreted tongues (14:19). There is no indication that he approved of lengthy tongues-speaking followed by interpretation. The public service of the church could get along with a minimum of tongues-speaking or even none at all (14:27–28), but teaching was always necessary.

2. The goals of teaching (14:20)

The second mention of the vocative "brethren" serves to conclude this section (cf. 14:6). Three simple commands are given.

First, do not become (*ginesthe*) children in spiritual perception. This word for "understanding" (*phresin*) is different from that previously used (*nous*). Paul definitely wanted to remove their ignorance over the purpose and importance of the spiritual gifts (cf. 12:1; 14:28). Children have a tendency to prefer that which is amusing rather than that which is helpful.

---

[12]The word *murious* is the largest number in the Greek language. It goes beyond ten thousand to countless myraids.

Second, "become infants" with respect to malice or wickedness. The word for "children" (*nēpiazete*) refers to babes in contrast with older children (*paidia*, 14:20a). Paul did not want them to have any knowledge or experience of sin through active participation.

Third, "become mature" or adults (*teleioi*; same word as "perfect" in 13:10) in spiritual perception. In their overestimation of tongues, they were as children in comparison with the mature Paul. They did not want to surrender their childish practices (cf. 13:11).

III. IN EVANGELISM (14:21–25)

In this section, Paul continued the contrast between tongues and prophecy. The first contrast is in their divine intent as signs, and the second can be seen in the response of the public to their general exercise.

A. As Signs (14:21–22)

1. The sign of tongues (14:21–22a)

Paul quoted from the Old Testament[13] to show that tongues-speaking in foreign languages was designed to be a sign to the unbelieving nation of Israel (14:21; cf. II Kings 18:26; Isa. 28:11–12). Through the Assyrians who were speaking Hebrew, God was trying to exhort His covenant people to repent, but they refused to obey. The conclusive analogy is introduced by the connective "wherefore" (14:22).

Tongues-speaking in the first century within the church was also designed as a sign to unbelievers, "to them that believe not." These unbelievers were Jews who constantly required signs (cf. 1:22; Matt. 16:1–4). On the day of Pentecost, the tongues-speaking was also used as a sign of God's rejection of national Israel (Acts 2:22–24, 32–36). At Corinth, the meeting place of the church was situated next door to the synagogue (Acts 18:7–8), thus unbelieving Jews would very likely attend the Christian services. To them, this sign was given and doubtlessly vanished when Jerusalem was destroyed by the Romans in A.D. 70. There

[13]The "law" can refer not only to the first five books, but also to the entire Old Testament canon (cf. John 10:34; Rom. 3:20).

is no indication that tongues was a sign of conversion or of a postconversion experience called "the baptism in the Holy Spirit." It was not a sign to them that believed.

2. The sign of prophecy (14:22b)

On the other hand, the gift of prophecy served as a sign to believers, primarily to Jewish believers since they could see in Gentile Christians who had the gift of prophecy the same operation of the Holy Spirit which was evident in the Old Testament prophets (14:22b). The value to the believers, of course, was in direct edification through understanding (cf. 14:3–4).

B. In Public Response (14:23–25)

Paul then theorized about two hypothetical situations to show the obvious superiority of prophecy as a means of evangelistic outreach.

1. To a church full of tongues-speakers (14:23)

Paul here refers to an officially called meeting of the church membership (cf. 11:18). If all spoke in tongues simultaneously, or one at a time, with or without interpretation, it would not make a difference. The unlearned (new believer or unsaved Gentile inquirer) and the unbelieving Jew would view the tongues-speakers as insane. The unbelieving Jews thought that the apostles were drunk (Acts 2:13–15), but the apostles gave them no legitimate cause for that criticism. This situation is entirely different. Although tongues were a sign, that significance was limited to three speakers (cf. 14:27).

2. To a church full of prophets (14:24–25)

If the regulations were followed (14:29–32), God would accomplish five results in the lives of the hearer. First, he would be convinced, or convicted, of his sin, guilt, and unbelief. The word "convinced" (*elegchetai*) is the same as that translated "reprove" (John 16:8). The Spirit of God convicts men of sin, righteousness, and judgment through His spokesmen. Second, he would be "judged by all." The spiritual man is the one who is able to judge all (cf. 2:15 — same word). Third, his true spiritual condition would be revealed to him (cf. Heb. 4:12). Fourth, he would repent and "worship God." Fifth, he would acknowledge the presence of God in their midst.

IV. IN THE CHURCH (14:26–40)

The third use of "brethren" and the question ("How is it then?") serve to introduce the final series of contrasts. Whenever the church met as an official body, Paul wanted the meeting to result in the edification of the entire group (14:26b). He also wanted the church to be marked by a variety of ministries and by a balance in the exercise of gifts (14:26a). Morris commented that the phrase "everyone" need not be pressed "to indicate that every member of the congregation always had something to contribute. But it does mean that any of them might be expected to take part in the service."[14]

A. Regulations (14:26–35)

Because of their ignorant abuse and misuse of the gifts, Paul placed strict limitations upon the order of the church services. To avoid confusion and competition and to promote edification, this was absolutely necessary.

1. For tongues (14:27–28)

Five restrictions are listed. First, no more than three people could speak in tongues in any one service (14:27a). This may indicate that only one tongues-speaker was forbidden to speak (note "let it be by two, or at the most by three"). Second, the two or three speakers were to speak one at a time ("by course"). No simultaneous speaking in competition or in unison was permitted.[15] Third, there was to be one interpreter for all three utterances. Interpretations by two or three men were not permitted. It is hard to determine whether the interpreter was one of the tongues-speakers (cf. 14:13) or a fourth individual. Fourth, there was to be no public tongues-speaking if a person with the gift of interpretation was not present. The guarantee of interpretation had to precede the actual tongues utterance. Fifth,

[14]Morris, *Corinthians,* p. 199.

[15]This shows that the gift of tongues in the church had a different purpose than that of the apostles who spoke simultaneously (Acts 2:4).

if no interpreter was present, then the tongues-speaker was to speak silently to himself and to God. If he could not add to the edification of the meeting, he was not to take away from it with an uninterpreted utterance.

2. For prophets (14:29–33)

Even though Paul had consistently set forth the superiority of prophecy to tongues, he nevertheless still imposed restrictions on that gift. In fact, six regulations are stated. First, only two or three prophets should be allowed to speak in one service. Again, this may mean that if only one prophet was present he was not permitted to speak. Second, the other prophets, or those with the gift of discerning spirits (12:10), were to judge the declarations. Old Testament prophets were likewise judged (Deut. 18:20–22). They probably had to determine what to do with what was revealed. Third, the gift of direct revelation was to take precedence over the exercise of discernment (14:30). Fourth, the prophets were to speak one at a time (14:31a). Fifth, the prophets were to have two main goals in their declarations and evaluations (cf. 14:3): that all, including themselves, might learn; and that all might be exhorted ("comfort" is the same word as "exhortation," parakaleō). Sixth, at all times the prophets should be in control of themselves and should act according to the regulations (14:32). Thus, he was "not overwhelmed by a compulsive external power which moved him automatically without his control."[16]

Apparently, the gifts were able to be used in the energy of the flesh as well as under the control of the Holy Spirit. God is a God of order and of peace; confusion and competition manifest an expression of the carnal flesh. Thus, God would never direct a tongues-speaker or a prophet to act contrary to the inscripturated regulations of the Word of God.

3. For women (14:34–35)

Many commentators[17] believe that the closing phrase of

[16]Boyer, World Like Ours, p. 134.

[17]Grosheide, Corinthians, p. 341; Hodge, Corinthians, p. 304; and Morris, Corinthians, p. 201.

verse 33 ("as in all churches of the saints") actually should begin the next verse. Earlier, Paul closed his exposition of the equality and the subordination of women with such a statement (11:16); now, he resumed a treatment of their vocal part in the service.

Four directives are delineated. First, the women were to be silent. There is a problem as to the extent of this silence. Earlier, Paul mentioned that women could pray or prophesy if properly attired and if they were in a right relationship to their husbands (11:5). Some believe that they could do this publicly, but not in a regular church service. However, it seems more likely that their silence referred to the ministry of discernment, to the asking of questions (cf. 14:35), and quite possibly to speaking in tongues. The verb "to speak" (*lalein*) is the same used for speaking in tongues; however, it must be admitted that Paul generally used the phrase "in a tongue" when referring to the charismatic gift.

Second, the women were to be in subjection to their husbands (14:34). The new dispensation did not abrogate that Old Testament principle. Apparently, women were not to speak in such a way as to force men to obey their declarations. Third, the women were to ask their husbands privately about the content of the prophecies, discernment, revelation, and interpreted tongues-utterances (14:35a). Fourth, women who tried to speak authoritatively in the church brought shame upon themselves and upon their husbands (14:35b; cf. 11:6).

B. Direct Revelation (14:36–40)

1. Channels of revelation (14:36)

In conclusion, Paul pointed out that although the Corinthians were a gifted church they were not to think that they were the only source or recipient of divine revelation. The phrase "the word of God" refers to the authoritative written and spoken divine directives. Paul was not talking about the spreading of the gospel message through various means (preaching, witnessing, etc.). In the days of the apostles, before the Biblical canon was completed, the gifts provided a way for God to communicate to His people.

2. Acceptance of revelation (14:37)

The Corinthians were to accept Paul's letter (especially chaps. 12—14) as the direct commandments of God. This shows that Paul knew that he was an authoritative spokesman for God. What he wrote was what God said. Both the prophet and the "spiritual" man (*pneumatikos*; probably an equivalent of the tongues-speaker[18]) were to acknowledge Paul's apostolic authority. Thus, all future oral declarations were to be seen and to be judged in the light of the epistle. The written Word of God is the final judge of all charismatic activities.

3. Rejection of revelation (14:38)

He added that the Corinthians had no justification for their ignorance on the subject of the spiritual gifts anymore. Any further ignorance simply indicated a carnal refusal to accept as binding what Paul had written.

4. Directives of revelation (14:39–40)

Paul then ended the chapter the way he began. Between the two gifts, he counseled them to covet the gift of prophecy (cf. 14:1). However, since the gift of tongues was a genuine gift and did have profit if properly exercised, they were not to forbid its practice. However, it must be noted that he did not charge them to covet tongues. As a revelatory gift, it had minimal value. In the time that God was revealing His Word (cf. 14:36), no mode of revelation could be forbidden. The questions for today are: Is divine revelation still going on? Is God adding to His Word (cf. Rev. 22:18–19)? If not, then the purpose of these gifts has ceased and with it their basis of existence.

Finally, all ministries of spiritual gifts and all church services should be done decently and in order (14:40). Love does not behave in an unseemly manner (*aschēmonei*, 13:5); loving members should do likewise (*euschēmonōs*). The concept of "in order" (*kata taxin*) conveys the rank and file of military discipline. Orderliness is the opposite of confusion (cf. 14:33).

---

[18]Grosheide, *Corinthians*, p. 344.

CALLED TO BE SAINTS

QUESTIONS FOR DISCUSSION

1. Do charismatic churches follow the regulations of this chapter?

2. Are women very prominent in the charismatic movement, as some claim?

3. Is there any justification from this section to make a distinction between uninterpreted tongues for private edification and interpreted tongues for public edification?

4. If someone would speak in tongues in your regular service, what would your pastor do? What would you do or think?

5. Should tongues-speakers be permitted to join the membership of a noncharismatic church?

6. Is there any tendency today to believe that God is still adding new revelation (visions, dreams, etc.)?

7. Can it be proved conclusively that tongues are for today? Can it be proved conclusively that they are not for today?

12

The Resurrection of the Body
I Corinthians 15

Greek thought accepted the immortality of the soul, but rejected the resurrection of the body. When Paul proclaimed future physical judgment guaranteed by the bodily resurrection of Christ, he was mocked by the Athenian philosophers (Acts 17:31–32). Some Corinthian pagans who were converted believed that Christ was resurrected but denied that they would be resurrected (15:12, 35). This pagan dichotomy, brought into the church, was heretical and had to be corrected. In so doing, Paul has provided believers with the classic chapter on the important subject of the resurrection of the body. The change in subject matter from the preceding section on gifts is clear, but abrupt. The familiar connective ("Now concerning") is missing, but he did use the same verb to introduce this section as he did the former ("I declare," *gnōrizō*; cf. "I give you to understand," 12:3).

I. THE NECESSITY OF CHRIST'S RESURRECTION (15:1–34)

Before dealing with the future resurrection of all men, Paul first had to show forth the necessity of the past resurrection of one man, namely Jesus Christ. The false teachers separated these two resurrections, but Paul argued that they were inseparably joined.

A. Essential Part of the Gospel (15:1–11)

1. Christ's resurrection is necessary for salvation (15:1–2)

Paul preached this truth in his original evangelization of Corinth (15:1a; cf. Acts 18:1–18). The Corinthians received that message and gained a justified standing before God by their position in the crucified, resurrected Christ (15:1b; cf. Rom. 5:1–10; II Cor. 1:24). In fact, their present progressive salvation was guaranteed by the resurrected Christ (sōzesthe, literally, "you are being saved"; cf. Rom. 5:10; Heb. 7:25).[1]

The conditional clause (introduced by "if") served as a warning to the false teachers and to their converts (cf. 15:12). Failure to "keep" (katechete) the total essence and effects of the gospel message would indicate that some of the professing Christians were not really saved in the first place. A saving faith is a persevering orthodox faith. The issue here is not faulty, immoral living, but incorrect doctrine. A "vain" belief (eikēi, "in vain") is a belief in a crucified, nonresurrected Christ, or a belief in a crucified, resurrected Christ who would not raise their physical bodies. Either heresy, revealed later in life, would show that a person did not properly understand the full implications of the gospel message when he made his original profession (cf. I John 2:18–19).

2. Christ's resurrection is part of the gospel definition (15:3–4)

Paul next stated that he simply transmitted or "delivered" what he had received directly from Christ (15:3a; cf. Gal. 1:11–12). He did not add or take away from its content. The definition is based upon the fourfold use of "that" (hoti). In so doing, two main facts (crucifixion and resurrection) were substantiated by two main proofs respectively (burial and appearances).

First, Christ's death was historical ("died"), redemptive and vicarious ("for our sins"), and planned ("according to the scriptures"; cf. Ps. 22; 69; Isa. 53; Zech. 12; Luke 22:37; 24:25; Acts 2:25–27; 13:24).[2] Second, His burial demonstrated the genuineness of His death. Third, Christ has been raised from the dead

---

[1]Some have suggested that the present tense may indicate the fact that new people were being saved daily through a belief in the resurrected Christ.

[2]Since Christ yielded His will to the Scriptures, so should all believers (cf. 14:37).

by the Father never to die again.[3] Here, the apostle emphasized
the fact ("rose"), the time ("third day"), and the divine plan ("according
to the scriptures"; cf. Ps. 16:10; Isa. 53:10–12; Jonah
1:17; Matt. 12:40). If Christ had been raised from the dead on
the second, fourth, or any succeeding day, that would have been
a remarkable, unprecedented achievement; but it also would
have declared Him to be a false prophet. He named the day of
His resurrection and He accomplished it on that specific day.
The religions of the world are all based upon the lives and the
teachings of their founders, but only Biblical Christianity rests
upon the death and resurrection of its Savior.

3. Christ's resurrection is proved by His appearances (15:5–7)

The fourth "that" introduces the proof for the bodily resur-

---

[3]The perfect passive indicative, used throughout this chapter (*egēgertai*; 15:2, 12,
13, 14, 16, 17, 20), shows that Christ was raised by another and that His resurrected state of existence is permanent. Christ did raise Himself from the grave
(John 10:17–18), but He was also raised by the Father (Acts 2:24). The persons
of the trinity always work together.

**The family tomb of the Herods, in Jerusalem. The stone that rolls to form a door
was a typical feature of Palestinian tombs.**

rection of Christ. Basically, the proof is twofold: the appearances of Christ (15:5–7) and the change in Paul's life (15:8–11). The apostle did not list all of the postresurrection appearances, but rather a sample selection which would be adequate to prove the reality of the resurrection.[4] The list shows that Christ appeared to individuals, small groups, and a large crowd; that He appeared at different times and in various places; and that He was seen, touched, and heard.

The six confirming testimonies include Cephas — or Peter (Mark 16:7; Luke 24:34), the twelve (Luke 24:36; John 20:19),[5] and the five hundred. Three statements are made about this group of five hundred (15:6). They all saw Him at one time.[6] In the approximate twenty-five years since that appearance, some had died, but the majority were still alive. Thus, their witness was available for cross-examination. The fourth witness was James, a half-brother of Christ who had not accepted the messiahship of Jesus during His earthly ministry (John 7:5; Acts 1:14; Gal. 1:19). The fifth witness, that of "all the apostles," probably refers to the events of the day of Christ's ascension into heaven (Acts 1:11).

4. Christ's resurrection changed Paul's life (15:8–11)

Paul used himself as the sixth and final witness (15:8; cf. Acts 9:1–6). He likened his experience to a fetal miscarriage or a violent, untimely entrance into life ("as of one born out of due time"). It probably refers to the fact that he saw Christ, was converted, and was commissioned as an apostle after the Savior had already gone into heaven. However, some agree with this

[4]He left out several mentioned in the Gospels, but he also included others not found there (e.g., James, the five hundred). Here is a complete list: to Mary Magdalene (John 20:14–18); to the women (Matt. 28:8–10); to Peter (Luke 24:34); to the two Emmaus disciples (Luke 24:13–31); to the ten apostles (Luke 24:36–43); to the eleven apostles (John 20:24–29); to seven disciples (John 21:1–23); to the five hundred (15:6); to James (15:7); to the eleven on the day of ascension (Acts 1:3–12); to Stephen (Acts 7:55); to Paul (Acts 9:3–6); and to John (Rev. 1:10–19).

[5]This shows that the words "the twelve" was a title assigned to the apostles as a group, and not to the actual number of individuals. With Judas gone, only ten or eleven apostles were present when Christ appeared.

[6]Mass hallucinations are unknown and impossible.

comment: "Paul thinks of himself here as an Israelite whose time to be born again had not come, nationally (cf. Matt. 23:29), so that his conversion by the appearing of the Lord in glory (Acts 9:3–6) was an illustration, or instance before the time of the future national conversion of Israel."[7]

Not only was the appearance of Christ the cause of Paul's regeneration, but he claimed that it was the basis of his apostleship (15:9–11). He sincerely believed that he was the least of the apostles because he had hated Christ and had persecuted Christians in his zealous Pharisaical life (cf. Gal. 1:13–16; Phil. 3:6; I Tim. 1:15). He knew that he now was a genuine apostle, equal to the others; but he also was aware of his personal unworthiness (cf. Gal. 1:1; II Cor. 11:5).

Beyond a shadow of a doubt, Paul knew that "the grace of God" was responsible for his calling (15:10). He humbly recognized that God's grace had accomplished its purpose in his life ("not in vain") and that "he labored more abundantly" than all of the other apostles. This was not proud boasting, but the declaration of a known fact. It could mean that he labored harder than any one of the apostles, but it may imply that he did more than all of them put together. From the Biblical record, it is true that he wrote more New Testament books, evangelized more territory, and started more churches than all of them. He gave God the praise for all that had been wrought through his life ("yet not I, but the grace of God").

Finally, he stated that all of the apostles preached the same message which he had just enumerated (15:11). Thus it did not matter to him who preached the gospel, just so they who heard it believed it in its entirety.

B. Linked to the Resurrection of All (15:12–19)

In this section, Paul logically debated that the resurrection of Christ and the resurrection of the human race could not be separated. To him, they were Siamese twins or two sides of the same coin. At Corinth, a doctrinal problem had developed. Some false teachers affirmed that Christ had been raised out of the sphere of the dead bodies (*ek nekrōn*; literally, "out of dead

---

[7]*Scofield Reference Bible*, p. 1226. Also Harry Ironside, *I Corinthians*, p. 467.

ones"), but they equally testified that there would be no resurrection of the "dead ones" themselves (15:12). To Paul, this was strict heresy. In three arguments he demonstrated what a denial of a future resurrection would lead to.

1. The denial of a resurrection means that Christ is still dead (15:13)

In the incarnation, Christ became man, and as man, He cannot be separated from the rest of the human race (cf. Heb. 2:14–15). Even though He was born of a virgin, He was still conceived and born; He grew as humans develop (Luke 2:52); He died physically as men die; and He rose again as men one day will.

2. The denial of a resurrection means that Paul's message was wrong (15:14–16)

It means that Paul's message was wrong in three respects. First, the message which he preached[8] was void, or empty of content ("vain," *kenon,* as a shell without a kernel). His words were empty, full of air and nothing else. Second, their faith was likewise empty or "vain" (*kenē*). Faith must be based upon fact (cf. 15:3-5). Biblical Christianity rests upon the acts of God within historical events. Third, Paul and his associates, including the other apostles, were false witnesses if Christ was not raised.[9] In fact, they incriminated God, because God was the one who sent them and told them what to preach ("testified of God" is literally "against God"; *kata tou theou*). If there is no resurrection, either past or future, then they were guilty of saying that God had done something which in reality He had not. At this point, Paul was arguing back from a future resurrection to a past one and from all men to one man (15:16). He wanted to show where a denial of the future resurrection would logically take a believer.

[8]"Preaching" (*kērygma*) does not refer to oral technique, but rather to the words of the proclamation.

[9]There is a subtle difference between a liar and a false witness. A liar tells as true what he knows is false. A false witness tells as true what he believes is true when really it is false.

3. The denial of resurrection means that the people were still unsaved (15:17–19)

First, if Christ was not raised their "faith" was useless or purposeless ("vain" is *mataia*, "futile or fruitless"). A dead Christ cannot do anything for anyone. Death is a major problem confronting the human race, thus to put faith in one who was overcome by death accomplishes nothing.

Second, they were still in their sins (15:17b). All men positionally are dead in sins (Eph. 2:1) and practically are dying in sins (John 8:21, 24). Although Christ died for sins, He was also raised in order that men might be made righteous and might be justified (Rom. 4:25). A crucified, nonresurrected Christ cannot deliver men from the penalty, power, and effects of sin.

Third, Christians who had died were thus unsaved and in Hades, perishing (15:18). The time to prepare for eternity is during one's life on earth; after death, it is too late. Consequently, they died with false hopes and with no opportunity to change their faith.

Fourth, Paul and his associates were men to be pitied ("miserable," *eleeinoteroi*) more than all others if Christ had not been raised. Why? Because for Him, they had given up everything (position in life including prestige, conveniences, and status) to travel all over the Roman world proclaiming a falsehood. They had gambled everything on Him and had lost!

C. Guarantees the Resurrection of All (15:20–28)

The negative tone of the preceding section is now offset by the positive assurance of this group of verses. The opening words ("but now") serve to mark that contrast and to form a transition between the two sections.

1. The resurrection was typified (15:20)

Using the principles of farming and the designation of an Old Testament feast, Paul expressed his belief in both the factual resurrection of Christ and the future resurrection of men. The sense of the verb "is risen" is that Christ is now in a permanent, risen state of existence as the result of an accomplished resurrection from the dead in the past, not that He is in the process of being raised.[10]

Earlier, Paul had referred to Christ as the Passover lamb, the fulfillment of the typology of the Passover feast (5:7–8). Now, Paul identified the Savior as "the firstfruits" (*aparchē*). In ancient times, the Jews were supposed to bring the first sheaf of the harvest to the tabernacle or temple as an offering to God (Lev. 23:10–11). This action consecrated the entire harvest, expressed their faith in the future harvest, and showed their thanksgiving for it. Christ's resurrection, thus, was a divine pledge that a future harvest of dead bodies would occur. In particular, this is a guarantee of the resurrection of the saved.[11]

2. *The resurrection is related to universal death (15:21–22)*

Adam was the agent of physical death (15:21a; cf. Gen. 2:17). Elsewhere, the apostle wrote: "Wherefore, as by one man sin entered into the world, and death by sin; and so death passed upon all men, for that all have sinned" (Rom. 5:12). By His incarnation, death, and resurrection, Christ then became the agent of physical resurrection (15:21b). The next verse continues the contrast in more detail (15:22). All men positionally are in Adam and therefore die physically (cf. Rom. 5:12–21). This is real and observable (note the present tense "die").

However, in Christ all will be made alive. This prediction allows for two possible interpretations. The prepositional phrase ("in Christ") may restrict this promise to believers only. However, Paul may be pointing out the fact that one effect of Christ's death and resurrection which extends to all men is that all will be delivered from physical death through the reception of a new resurrection body. But the destiny of that resurrection body (heaven or the lake of fire) is determined by one's conscious rejection or acceptance of God's revealed truth, including the gospel message (Rom. 1:18 — 3:31). It is predicted elsewhere that all will be raised from the dead (Dan. 12:2; John 5:29–29; Acts 17:31).

[10]The latter would be indicated by the present passive indicative.

[11]Paul uses this terminology for Christians (cf. I Thess. 4:13–14).

3. The resurrection will be in stages (15:23–24)

Although all will be raised from the dead, they will not be raised at the same time. Each man will be resurrected in his own order (15:23a). The word "order" (*tagmati*) is a military term, indicating the separation of soldiers into detachments for marching in reviews or in battle. Three orders are expressed.

The first occurred nineteen hundred years ago when "Christ the firstfruits" was raised from the tomb. The term "firstfruits" may refer exclusively to Christ as the total fulfillment of the Old Testament feast typology; but it may also include those bodies of dead saints who were raised at the time of His resurrection (Matt. 27:52–53). Whether those bodies were raised to an immortal, incorruptible state or not is really incidental; the fact is that they were raised and that event was a divine guarantee of a future resurrection.

The second order is indicated by the chronological connective "afterward" (*epeita*). At the "coming" (*parousia*) of Christ, the redeemed will be resurrected. Elsewhere, this is called the first resurrection (Rev. 20:5–6).[12]

The third order is designated by the phrase, "Then cometh the end."[13] After the millennial reign of Christ, the second resurrection will take place (15:24; cf. Rev. 20:5, 11–15). This is the resurrection of all of the unsaved dead of all ages. The "end" is further defined in two ways (indicated by the double use of "when" (*hotan*). It is the time when Christ delivers the kingdom over which He has ruled to the Father and when He has rendered inoperative ("put down" *katargēsēi*) every foe, both angelic and human (cf. Eph. 6:11–12; Rev. 20:7–10).

4. The resurrection eliminates the enemy, death (15:25–26)

The "reign" of Christ will continue until all enemies are in

---

[12]Dispensational pretribulationists believe that the first resurrection is in three stages: Christ, the church dead before the tribulation, and both the tribulation martyrs and the Old Testament saints after the tribulation before the millennium. Posttribulations believe that the saints of all ages will be raised at the same time.

[13]Some believe that "the end" does not refer to another resurrection, but rather to the end of the world order. Thus, to deny the reality of a future resurrection is to deny the end of earth history.

total subjection to Him (15:25). The final joint demonic and human rebellion will occur after Satan has been released from his imprisonment within the abyss and after he has deceived the human race once more (cf. Rev. 20:1-3, 7-10). After Christ puts down that futile insurrection, He will destroy or render inoperative (*katargeitai*; cf. 15:25) the last enemy, physical death, by raising all of the unsaved dead who must then appear before Him at the great white throne. They will be subsequently sent to the second death, namely the lake of fire (Rev. 20:11-15).

5. The resurrection results in total subjection (15:27-28)

The dominion over the earth which Adam lost through his sin was regained by Christ through His incarnation, death, and resurrection (15:27a; cf. Gen. 1:26; Ps. 8:6; Heb. 2:5-8). The phrase "all things" (*panta*) includes physical death but naturally excludes the Father who decreed the subjection (15:27b). When earth history is concluded and eternity begins, even the incarnate Son of God will be in subjection to the Father (15:28). Although the Son is equal to the Father in divine essence, the former will continue to manifest His identification with the human race throughout eternity.[14] Since Christ was raised by the Father, His subordination to the Father as the God-man will serve as a fitting example to the resurrected redeemed and to the holy angels.

D. Provides Spiritual Motivation (15:29-34)

1. For baptism (15:29)

To the apostle, the resurrection was necessary to fulfill the meaning of water baptism. Baptism involves an identification with Christ in His physical death and resurrection (Rom. 6:3-5) and with other Christians who have so identified themselves, both in the past and in the present. Thus, baptism would lose its meaning if Christ had not been raised from the dead in the past or if the dead will not be raised in the future.[15] Although Paul

[14]Johnson, however, stated: "When he delivers up the administration of the earthly kingdom to the Father, then the triune God will reign as God and no longer through the incarnate Son." *The Wycliffe Bible Commentary*, p. 1257.

[15]Over thirty different interpretations have been given for this difficult verse. The Mormons practice proxy baptism in which the living are baptized for dead ancestors who were not Mormons.

had divorced baptism from the gospel message earlier (1:17), the ordinance was necessary as an initiatory rite of obedience and of fellowship.

2. For possible martyrdom (15:30–32)

Paul had willingly risked his life because of his belief in Christ's resurrection and of his hope for his own. He acknowledged that his life was presently threatened at Ephesus (15:30; cf. 16:9; Acts 19:23–41). The rejoicing of the Corinthians in the resurrection of Christ contributed to Paul's perseverance; however, he saw no advantage in his human predicament if they denied what he stood for (15:31; cf. 15:21, 19).

He died daily (15:31b)[16] in that he was always subjected to the possibility of physical harm and martyrdom. The dangers that threatened him were real and constant (cf. II Cor. 1:8–10). In fact, he may have been thrown into the arena to be torn apart by wild animals ("beasts"). However, this may be a symbolic reference to conflicts with pagan religionists in Ephesus (note "after the manner of men"; cf. II Peter 2:12; Jude 10). His conclusive argument is clear and concise: ". . . what advantageth it me, if the dead rise not?" If there is no general resurrection of the dead, then there is no specific resurrection for him. If death is the end of physical existence, then Paul reasoned that a life of sin was better than a life of holiness (cf. Isa. 22:13).

3. For holy living (15:33–34)

In fact, their insensitivity to the doctrine of a future resurrection had actually harmed their present spiritual experience in six ways. First, they were being led astray by false teachers (15:33a). The word for "deceived" (planasthe) is taken from the word for wandering planets in the sky. Second, they had forgotten that wrong doctrine would corrupt good behavior (15:33b). Paul here quoted a familiar maxim, accepted by both the pagan and the Christian worlds. The word "communications" (homiliai) originally meant social intercourse or fellowship, then came to designate the speeches and conversation that developed from that friendliness.

Third, they were carnally drunk in their worldliness, and

---

[16]The critical text places this phrase at the beginning of the verse.

needed to become righteously sober (15:34a). Fourth, they were actively sinning in both doctrinal and moral error and needed to stop their practice. Fifth, they were unconcerned about the lost, for those who had "not the knowledge of God" (15:34b). In their debates about the resurrection of the physical dead, they had forgotten that there were men around them who were spiritually dead. If these unsaved men did not repent, then they would have to face Christ after their resurrection at the great white throne judgment. Sixth, they were bringing shame to their spiritual life and testimony (15:34c; cf. 4:14; 6:5).

II. THE NATURE OF THE RESURRECTION (15:35–58)

After pointing out the necessity of the resurrection, Paul felt forced to expound the nature of the resurrection body. He anticipated two questions from his opponents (15:35). The first dealt with the method of resurrection ("How . . . ?") and the second with the characteristics of the body itself ("With what body . . . ?"). The critics doubtless thought about many difficult situations which would tend to make resurrection improbable, if not impossible: How could life come out of cremated ash? What about a person eaten by a shark? What about those who died in infancy? What about the deformed? To such mockers, Paul spoke directly: "Thou fool." Morris commented that ". . . its bluntness makes clear Paul's view of the worthlessness of such arguments."[17]

A. The Resurrection Body (15:36–50)

1. The resurrection body will be related to the natural body (15:36–38)

The foolishness of the critic was caused by a failure to observe some of the principles underlying the growth of living plants. Nature teaches that life (a living plant) comes out of the death of the seed in the ground (15:36). It also shows a continuation of the life principle from the seed to the plant. The paradox is that the plant is "quickened," or made alive (*zōopoieitai;* cf. 15:22), by the death of the seed.

Also, what comes out of the ground is not the same as that which went into the earth (15:37). A farmer does not sow a stalk

[17]Leon Morris, *The First Epistle of Paul to the Corinthians,* p. 223.

of corn, but rather a mere kernel. However, what comes out of the ground is based upon and related to what went into the earth. To get wheat, one must sow grains of wheat; to get corn, one must sow kernels of corn. You cannot grow corn by sowing wheat or barley.

God has so designed the genetic code that men can trust the relationship that exists between seed and plant (15:38).[18] What men attribute to evolutionary natural law, Paul saw as the superintending, sovereign plan of God controlling His creation. The analogies of the seed-plant relationships to the natural-resurrection body should be obvious.

2. *The resurrection body will be consistent with the principles of creation (15:39–41)*

First, there are differences in flesh (15:39). The flesh (skin, bone, blood) of human beings is different from that of the animals which in turn is different from that of the fish which in turn is different from that of birds. There is a continuity of life within a kind (Gen. 1:11), but not between kinds.[19] It does not follow, however, that a resurrection within the human race implies a resurrection within the other kinds (animals, fish, birds).

Second, there are differences in bodies (15:40a). The contrast between the celestial, or heavenly, and the terrestrial bodies probably refers to the difference between angelic beings and human beings, although it could point out a distinction between the stars and the planets with their moons.

Third, there are differences in glory (15:40b–41). The contrast between celestial and terrestrial bodies, if referring to persons, could manifest the radiance of angelic beings with that of humans (cf. Rev. 18:1); or it could refer to the production of their own light by the sun and stars in contrast to the reflected light of the planets and moons. Astronomers have been able to measure the size and the respective intensity of light of the sun,

---

[18]The present tense for "gives" shows that God actively and daily determines the life cycle of plants. The aorist tense for "pleased" shows that He acts according to His plan devised in eternity past.

[19]This incidentally is a strong argument against the evolutionary hypothesis.

the moon, and the countless stars. In every case, the brilliance varies from star to star.

3. The resurrection body will be different from the natural body (15:42–44)

The various differences in flesh, body, and glory provided the background for Paul's statement of analogy: "So also is the resurrection of the dead" (15:42). Using the metaphor of farming (cf. 15:26–37), he pointed out a fourfold contrast between the physical body which a person has for present earthly existence, and the resurrection body, which he will have for future heavenly existence (15:42–44).

First, the physical nature "is sown in corruption" but "raised in incorruption." The present body is subject to disease and illness, but the future body will be immune from such attacks.

Second, it "is sown in dishonor" (*atimiāi*), but "raised in glory." A corpse has no rights; it is not an object of praise or jealousy, but the new body will manifest a superior existence far beyond human imagination (cf. Rom. 8:18–23).

Third, it "is sown in weakness," but "raised in power" (*dynamei*). The present body has so many physical limitations. It needs rest and sleep, food, water, air, and protection from adverse environments; but the resurrection body will have an eternal self-sufficiency within it decreed by God. There is no indication that it will need sleep or food.

Fourth, it "is sown a natural body," but "raised a spiritual body." The natural body is a "soulish" body (*psychikon*), a body adapted to the soul of man and suited to present earthly life in all of its aspects (sex, reproduction, social relationships; cf. the *psychikos* man, 2:14). On the other hand, the spiritual body is not immaterial or pure spirit. Rather, it is a body which is adapted to the spirit or that which corresponds to the image of God in man. Today, the spirit is hampered by a soulish body, but in eternity, the body will be dominated by the spirit. The Greeks attempted to make a distinction between the corruptible body and the incorruptible soul, but Paul showed that the real difference was between the natural body (corruptible) and the spiritual body (incorruptible and resurrection).

4. The resurrection body will reflect the differences between Adam and Christ (15:45–49)

Five contrasts are given (15:45–47).[20] First, Christ is called "the last Adam" over against "the first man Adam." Two headships are immediately established: one over the natural body and one over the resurrection body.

Second, Adam became a living soul by the infusion of the breath of God into the lifeless body made of dust (Gen. 2:7), but Christ became a lifegiving[21] spirit by His resurrection from the dead through the Father's power which gave the Son authority to raise others (John 5:26–29).

Third, in the original creation, Adam received a "natural" (psychikon) body, but in the resurrection, Christ received a "spiritual" (pneumatikon) body.

Fourth, Adam was out "of the earth" (gēs) with an "earthy" (choikos) body, but Christ is the "Lord from heaven." Although this latter reference might be to the incarnation, it probably refers to the second coming. Men today look back to Adam's earthy origin for their natural bodies, but they should look up to Christ for the heavenly origin of their resurrection bodies. Fifth, Adam is called "the first man" and Christ is named "the second man."

Having declared the two headships of humanity, Paul then pointed out the principle that like produces like (15:48–49). The likeness can be seen in the use of the qualitative "as" (hoios) and the quantitative "such" (toioutoi), and the contrast between the singular and the plural. All men have received their earthy, corruptible bodies from one man, Adam; and all redeemed men will receive their heavenly, incorruptible bodies from one man, namely Christ. The guarantee is that all believers will bear "the image of the heavenly" Christ just as they have borne the "image (eikona) of the earthy" Adam (cf. Phil. 3:21; I John 3:2). Just as all men have natural bodies with distinct, personal characteristics (fingerprints, height, color), so all believers will have resurrection bodies with distinguishing marks of personal identity. We

---

[20]Note the transition into this new thought by the repeated use of "so" (houtōs, 15:42; cf. 15:45).

[21]Same word as "make alive" (15:22) and "quickened" (15:36).

will not all look like Christ or like each other, and yet we will all have spiritual bodies with the same properties.

5. *The resurrection body will be adapted to life in eternity (15:50)*

The "flesh and blood" body, or man's present human nature (Gal. 1:16; Heb. 2:14) has been designed for life on this planet. It can breathe the surrounding air and eat its food. This body, however, has not been fabricated for heavenly life in the eternal presence of God. Corruption cannot inherit what is designed for incorruption. This is why God must change the human body from a natural state to a spiritual state.

B. The Translated Body (15:51–53)

1. *The mystery of the translation (15:51)*

The exclamatory "Behold" introduces this new section. In it, Paul wanted to reveal the fact that some believers would receive a spiritual body apart from death and resurrection. Although two ancient saints had been caught up into heaven apart from death (Enoch, Heb. 11:5; and Elijah, II Kings 2:11), the Old Testament believer knew that he would die and that he would be resurrected when the Messiah came at the last day (Job 19:25–27; John 11:24). Through Paul, however, was revealed the "mystery" that New Testament saints could fully expect that Christ would return in their lifetime and would change their natural state immediately into a spiritual one. Thus, living believers in a "flesh and blood" condition would also have to be translated into that type of body suitable for the eternal kingdom of God. This was Paul's own personal hope (note the inclusion of himself in "we").[22]

2. *The quickness of the translation (15:52a)*

Three prepositional phrases (indicated by *en*, translated as "in" and "at") show the quickness of the translation for living saints. A "moment" (*atomōi*) is that part of time which cannot be divided anymore. The scientific word "atom" comes from this word. The "twinkling of an eye" must be contrasted with the

[22]Paul did not believe that Christ *would* come in his lifetime, only that He *could* come. If he believed the former, then the apostle was grossly mistaken.

"blinking" of an eye. The former refers to the time it takes to cast a glance. The "last trump" is not the same as the seventh trumpet of the Revelation judgments (cf. Rev. 11:5); rather, it is a military term. In the Roman army encampments, trumpets were sounded to cause the soldiers to wake up, to pack up gear, to fall into line, and to march away. The "last trump" for Christians thus is their call to come up into heaven.

3. The order of the translation (15:52b)

The order of the change from the natural state to the spiritual body is pointed out by the explanatory connective "for" (15:52b; cf. I Thess. 4:13–18). First, there will be the "sounding of the trump" of God (I Thess. 4:16). Next, the real self of the believer which has been in Christ's presence since his death will be joined to a resurrected, incorruptible body. Finally, each living Christian will be "changed" directly into a translated, incorruptible body. Both groups of believers receive the same type of eternal body, but they get it in two different ways.

4. The necessity for the translation (15:53)

The change for both groups is an absolute necessity (15:53; "must" comes from *dei*). The "corruptible, mortal" body of a person which is subject to disease and to death must be replaced by a body which will never get sick nor die.

C. The Victorious Bodies (15:54–58)

The change of the body from a natural to a spiritual state involves the believer in an ultimate triumph. In it, Paul saw five results. First, it fulfills prophecy (15:54; cf. Isa. 25:8).

Second, it involves victory over death (15:55; cf. Hos. 13:14).[23] Death has hurt the living as well as the departed, and from mere natural observation, it has won over every human being. But resurrection will reverse all of that (cf. Rev. 21:4–5).

Third, it involves victory over sin and the law (15:56). The wages of sin is death, and all men have sinned by failure to live according to God's commandments (Rom. 3:23; 6:23). Fourth, it is a divine victory (15:57). Its source is God, its nature is that of a

---

[23]The words "death" and "grave" come from the same Greek word —*thanatos*.

gift, and its means is the death and resurrection of Christ. The believer should be thankful not only for deliverance from the second death in the eternal lake of fire, but also for the hope of a new body.

Fifth, it should promote faithful, holy living in the present life of a believer (15:58). It should give him stedfastness or a stable purposefulness in his living (cf. 7:37). He should be unmoveable, not vascillating between carnality and spirituality. He should be exceedingly zealous to do God's work out of gratitude for all that the Lord has done for him. He should be positive and optimistic in his outlook, especially since he has the promise of a new body. This hope should eliminate depression, self-pity, and a defeatistic-pessimistic viewpoint of life.

QUESTIONS FOR DISCUSSION

1. Is there enough reference made to the resurrection of Christ in gospel tracts and evangelistic messages? If not, what may the reason be?

2. Can a person be genuinely saved by believing only in a Christ who was crucified for him?

3. In addition to the postresurrection appearances, what other proofs exist for the bodily resurrection of Christ?

4. What is the difference between bragging and giving proper praise to God for accomplishments?

5. Will I know my loved ones in heaven? Is there any real value in answering that question?

6. Should a Christian be cremated? Would it be proper for him to donate his body to science or his organs to some needy recipient?

7. Are contemporary funerals Christian? Can anything be done to improve the act of burial?

13

Closing Concerns
I Corinthians 16

With the major moral and doctrinal issues behind him, Paul now turned to some final, personal concerns. This closing section certainly illustrates the human side of Biblical inspiration in that private desires and divine directives blend into the same expressions.[1] In fact, Morris called this final chapter "a little 'chatty' section."[2] Two of the closing matters probably stemmed from their letter to him (16:1, 12; cf. 7:1), but they are treated as typical closing subjects with which Paul normally ended his epistles.

I. THE COLLECTION (16:1–4)

The familiar connective ("Now concerning"; cf. 7:1, 25; 8:1; 12:1; 16:12) shows the transition from the subject of the resurrection to that of the collection. Three important features of it were given.

A. It Was to Be a Joint Project (16:1)

It was to be taken for other "saints" (cf. Gal. 6:10), probably for the poor believers at Jerusalem. Their poverty was caused by a famine (Acts 11:27–30), by persecution (Acts 8:1; I Thess. 2:14; Heb. 10:34), by the sale of their private property (Acts 4:34), and by their mere economic and social status. Regardless,

---

[1]The human writer was an active participant, not a passive stenographer. The theory of mechanical, verbal dictation cannot account for the warm human touches of this section.

[2]Leon Morris, *The First Epistle of Paul to the Corinthians*, p. 236.

when one part of the body of Christ suffers, then all other members should compassionately help out (cf. 1:9; 12:26). Paul had "instructed the churches" both of Galatia (16:1) and of Macedonia (II Cor. 8:1; 9:2) to assist and they had consented (cf. Rom. 15:24–27). Now the apostle wanted the Corinthians to get involved as well.

B. It Involved Advance Preparation (16:2)

Each believer ("every one of you"), whether rich or poor (cf. II Cor. 8:2), was to share. The amount to be given was in direct proportion to God's financial blessing upon their lives. The word "prospered" literally means a "good journey" (*euodōtai*). The money was to be saved, or stored. Some have suggested that each believer was to maintain a private fund at home,[3] but it appears more likely that what was saved at home was to be brought to the church each Sunday to be stored until Paul came.

The fact that it was to be collected each Sunday shows that the church formally met only once a week. Both the Jewish feast of firstfruits (Lev. 23:10–11) and the feast of Pentecost (cf. Acts 2) occurred on the first day of the week. Although Israel had celebrated the Sabbath as its day of worship, the church looked to the day of Christ's resurrection as its official meeting day (John 20:19, 26; Acts 20:7; Rev. 1:10). To the Christian, the Sabbath was abrogated by Christ's death (Col. 2:16). The advance storage of funds was designed to prevent any last-minute "gatherings" (*logias*; same word as in 16:1). Paul wanted the money to be "in hand" by the time he arrived.

C. It Involved the Sending of Messengers (16:3–4)

These emissaries were to be selected and approved by the church membership. The phrase "by letters"[4] can go either with "approve" or "send," probably the latter. It was Paul's plan to send the church-approved messengers with the relief collection and with his apostolic credentials to Jerusalem. Paul had no intention of taking the money himself lest people misjudge his

[3]F. W. Grosheide, *Commentary on the First Epistle to the Corinthians,* p. 398, and A. T. Robertson, *Word Pictures in the New Testament,* 4:200.

[4]Note that "your" is in italics. The word does not appear in the Greek.

motivations (cf. chap. 9). The apostle then injected the possibility ("if it be meet") that he might accompany the messengers rather than follow them (16:4). However, the Biblical record seems to indicate that they did not go with him (cf. Acts 20:1–4 where no one from Corinth is mentioned).

II. TRAVEL PLANS (16:5–12)

In this section, Paul discussed the travel plans of three persons: himself, Timothy, and Apollos.

A. For Paul (16:5–9)

Some of Paul's critics thought that he would not return to Corinth (4:18), but he announced clearly that he would visit them (16:5a; cf. 4:19–21; II Cor. 1:23). His plans involved three stages.

1. Ephesus to Macedonia (16:5)

He planned to pass through the Roman province of Macedonia in northern Greece, stopping off at the various churches in Philippi, Thessalonica, and Berea. This would serve not only as an opportunity for renewed fellowship and ministry, but it would enable him to receive the Macedonian relief money and it would give the Corinthian church more time in which to fulfill its financial commitment.

2. Macedonia to Corinth (16:6–7)

Instead of a brief visit, he announced that he desired to spend the winter months with them. He probably shocked them by telling them that he would accept their financial support for the next leg of his journey (16:6b; cf. 9:15). He informed them that he could not visit them now to deal with their various problems. Since he could not leave Ephesus, he sent this authoritative letter to answer their needs; however, he reaffirmed his hope in a future visit (16:7). Recognizing the sovereignty of God, he committed his travel plans to the will of God ("if the Lord permit"; cf. James 4:13–15). It *was* the Lord's will, and Paul was able to stay there for three months (Acts 20:1–3).

3. At Ephesus (16:8–9)

The apostle labored for three years in that Asian city (Acts 20:31), but he here put a time limit upon his ministry ("until Pentecost"). His reason for staying was that God had "opened to him a great and effectual door" for proclaiming the gospel. On the second missionary journey God had forbidden Paul to preach in Asia (Acts 16:6), but on the third journey God had opened the closed door (Rev. 3:7–8). Paul knew that his responsibility was to go through opened doors, not to fret about closed doors. He also knew that it was God who did the opening and the closing (II Cor. 2:12; Col. 4:3). From the base at Ephesus, all of Asia was evangelized (Acts 19:10). Many people were converted and several churches were established.

It was an effectual work in that God used His Word to penetrate the sinful hearts of men (cf. Heb. 4:12, same word translated as "powerful"). However, wherever God is working, Satan will be there to oppose. Ephesus was no exception (16:9b). The adversaries certainly included the pagan silversmiths and the idolatrous worshipers of Diana (cf. Acts 19:23–41).

B. For Timothy (16:10–11)

When Paul had heard about the problems at Corinth, he sent Timothy to deal with the situation; however, the young associate must have traveled by land through Macedonia first (4:17). Paul expected the letter, which would go directly across the Aegean Sea, to arrive before Timothy. This is why the apostle prepared the church for the visit of the young man of God (16:10a.).

He gave the church four specific instructions as to their proper reception of his representative. First, they were not to cause him any "fear" or anxiety. By nature, Timothy was timid and, in addition, he was very young (cf. I Tim. 4:12).[5] Second, they were to treat him as a co-worker with Paul and with God (cf. 3:9).

Third, they were not to despise him (16:11a). To despise means to think absolutely nothing about a person. Paul knew that the carnal Corinthians could take advantage of Timothy's

---

[5]Some years after Paul wrote this letter, he still regarded Timothy as a young man.

youthful sincerity, deep humility, and lack of experience. Fourth, they were to give him a peaceful and financial farewell (16:11b; "conduct" is the same word as "bring," 16:6). Thus, Paul fully expected Timothy to rejoin him at Ephesus before the apostle himself departed.

C. For Apollos (16:12)

The words "as touching" come from the same connective (*peri de*) used to point out the various questions submitted in the church's letter to Paul. Apparently, the church asked about Apollos and his next visit to their city. Maybe they wanted him to come to cope with their ecclesiastical problems. In any case, Paul respected Apollos and regarded him as a genuine brother, not as a threat to his ministry (cf. 3:4). In fact, the apostle wanted Apollos to return to Corinth with the brethren (perhaps the church messengers, 16:17). However, Apollos did not want to go at that particular time. This fact shows that Paul did not impose his apostolic authority upon Apollos, that Apollos was aware of the delicate situation in Corinth, and that he did not want to interfere with Paul's counsel and direction. Apollos wanted to return, but he desired a more opportune time for his visit (16:12b).

III. FINAL INSTRUCTIONS (16:13–18)

In this section, Paul gave final instructions to the church about three groups.

A. The Church (16:13–14)

Five imperatives are given to the church.[6] The first four are actually military terms (cf. Eph. 6:10–17). First, watch or be on the alert (cf. Matt. 24:42; 25:13). This command usually has reference to the second coming of Christ. Second, "stand fast in the faith." Paul did not want them to be moved by false doctrines or loose morals. Third, "quit you like men." These four words are the translation of one Greek word (*andrizesthe*). The apostle wanted them to grow up, to mature, and not to be childish. Fourth, "be strong." In the face of satanic and human persecu-

---

[6]The first four are second person singular commands and the sixth is a third person imperative.

tion, Paul wanted them to be bold. Fifth, in relationship to the family of God, "love" (cf. Col. 3:14).

B. The House of Stephanas (16:15–16)

1. *Its contribution to the church (16:15)*

This family composed some of the few people that Paul baptized in the city of Corinth (1:16). Paul pointed out two outstanding characteristics of this family. First, they constituted the first converts of the apostle's evangelistic efforts in the southern Grecian province of Achaia, with its chief cities of Athens and Corinth. They may have actually been the first believers at either city, or else this expression may mean that they were the first total family to come to Christ even though individuals in that region had been saved before them. Second, they had self-appointed themselves to the ministry of serving others, probably financially as well as spiritually. The word "addicted" comes from *etaxan,* a term used for "ordination."

2. *Its acceptance by the church (16:16)*

The purpose of Paul's appeal ("I beseech") is indicated by the word "that." He wanted the church to be submissive to such experienced, humble servants and to every other person who assisted and worked with Paul (e.g., Timothy, 16:10–11).

C. The Church Messengers (16:17–18)

Stephanas, Fortunatus, and Achaicus were probably the representatives sent by the Corinthian church with the letter of inquiry (cf. 7:1). When they came, Paul rejoiced over them in three areas.

1. *Their presence (16:17a)*

He rejoiced over their actual presence ("coming," *parousia;* literally, "to be beside"). Their fellowship was coveted and loved by the apostle.

2. *Their gift (16:17b)*

He rejoiced over the gift of money which they brought to him. It may be that the church had sent a gift along with the

Fountainhead of Peirene, at Corinth.

letter or it may mean that the three had given out of their own pockets to make up for the deficiency in the church's giving.

3. Their refreshment (16:18)

He rejoiced because they had refreshed both his spirit and that of the church. The word "refreshed" (*anepausan*) is the same word translated "give rest" in Christ's admonition: "Come unto me, all ye that labour and are heavy laden, and I will give you rest" (Matt. 11:28). Thus, the three messengers refreshed Paul by helping to bear the burden of the apostle's work.

Paul finally charged the church to recognize fully (*epiginōs-kete*, "acknowledge") the spiritual contributions of the three messengers and to give them due appreciation and honor (16:18b).

IV. CLOSING REMARKS (16:19–24)

The epistle ends in a typical Pauline fashion. Both greetings and a benediction are extended to the readers, but in between, a warning is inserted.

A. Greetings (16:19–21)

Six various groups or individuals are mentioned as the source of greetings.

1. From the churches of Asia (16:19a)

These churches were established as the direct result of Paul's open door of evangelism in Ephesus (16:8–9; cf. Acts 19:10). They included Smyrna, Pergamos, Thyatira, Sardis, Philadelphia, Laodicea, Colosse, Hierapolis, and possibly others (cf. Col. 4:13; Rev. 1:11).

2. From Aquila and Priscilla (16:19b)

It was in the home of this couple that Paul found lodging and work when he first came to Corinth (Acts 18:2–3). When the apostle left Corinth, they journeyed with him to Ephesus where they were instrumental in leading Apollos to a saving knowledge of Christ (Acts 18:18–19, 24–28). This couple then labored in Corinth for eighteen months just as Paul had and probably knew most of the church members.

3. From the church at Ephesus (16:19c)

The local church at Ephesus apparently met in the house of Aquila and Priscilla and it likewise sent greetings. Later on, the couple returned to Rome, and again the church in that city met in their house (Acts 18:2; Rom. 16:3–5). Consequently, the couple assisted spiritually and financially in the founding of three churches: Corinth, Ephesus, and Rome.

4. From all the brethren (16:20a)

All the brethren associated with Paul in the formal ministry extended their greetings.

5. From the Corinthians themselves (16:20b)

The members of the Corinthian church were to greet each other with a sincere "kiss of holiness" (cf. Rom. 16:16; II Cor. 13:12; I Thess. 5:26). Peter called it "a kiss of love" (I Peter 5:14). Based upon synagogue tradition, the kiss involved men to men and women to women. Instead of schism, there was to be love.

6. From Paul (16:21)

Ordinarily, the apostle used an amanuensis or a secretary to write the epistle (cf. Rom. 16:22), but he always wrote the concluding greetings to convey the personal touch and to prove that it was an authentic Pauline letter (Col. 4:18; II Thess. 2:2; 3:17).

B. Warning (16:22)

1. Its essence

In a church marked by moral impurity and doctrinal error, Paul knew that there might be unsaved members; thus he gave a sober warning. He ended the second epistle in the same way: "Examine yourselves, whether ye be in the faith, prove your own selves. Know ye not your own selves, how that Jesus Christ is in you, except ye be reprobates?" (II Cor. 13:5). The Galatian church heard similar words (Gal. 1:6–9).

2. Its basis

The basis of his warning was a lack of "love" (*philei*) for Jesus Christ. Such absence is a sign that a person has never been regenerated (cf. I John 3:14; 4:19–20). The judgment for disobeying the warning is contained in the word "Anathema." Elsewhere, it is translated as "accursed" (Gal. 1:8–9). Such deliberate hypocrisy will lead to the lake of fire.

3. Its urgency

A period should actually come after "Anathema" and before "Maran-atha." There is no grammatical connection between the two words. The word "Maran-atha"[7] is an Aramaic expression, used very early by Palestinian Christians and accepted by Greek believers without translation. In this context, it could have three possible translations. First, it could refer to Christ's incarnation, meaning "Our Lord has come." Second, it could be a prophetic declaration, "Our Lord is coming." Or third, it could be a prayer: "Our Lord, come" (cf. Rev. 22:20). The latter two seem to be more probable.

[7]"*Mar*" means "Lord"; "*an*" is "our"; and "*atha*" is the verb "to come."

C. Blessing (16:23–24)

Paul always exalted "the grace of Christ" (16:23; cf. 15:10; Eph. 2:8). This blessing is of moderate length. A shorter form (Col. 4:18) and a longer form (II Cor. 13:14) can be found elsewhere.

The apostle ended the letter by expressing his love for all genuine Corinthian believers. Although they were carnal and ignorant, they were still positionally acceptable in Jesus Christ. If Paul could love them, then they should be able to love one another.

QUESTIONS FOR DISCUSSION

1. Should Christians give to worthy projects through a local church only?

2. Should Christians participate in secular relief funds for the poor of the world? In supporting the poor, should they give only to poor believers?

3. Can this passage be used to teach storehouse tithing? Does God require more than a tenth of one's income?

4. Should pastors and Christian workers follow the example of Paul and avoid becoming treasurers of money?

5. How can believers today distinguish between open and closed doors?

6. How can human plans and the will of God be blended into one purpose?

7. Do believers today express their love and concern for each other in a visible way? If not, what can be done to improve the situation?

Selected Bibliography

Boyer, James B. *For a World Like Ours*. Grand Rapids: Baker Book House, 1971.

Godet, Frederick L. *Commentary on the First Epistle of St. Paul to the Corinthians*. Grand Rapids: Zondervan Publishing House, 1957.

Grosheide, F. W. *Commentary on the First Epistle to the Corinthians*. Grand Rapids: Wm. B. Eerdmans Publishing Co., 1974.

Hobbs, Herschel H. *The Epistles to the Corinthians*. Grand Rapids: Baker Book House, 1960.

Hodge, Charles. *An Exposition of the First Epistle to the Corinthians*. Grand Rapids: Wm. B. Eerdmans Publishing Co., 1974.

Ironside, H. A. *Addresses on the First Epistle to the Corinthians*. New York: Loizeaux Brothers, 1955.

Johnson, S. Lewis. "The First Epistle to the Corinthians," *The Wycliffe Bible Commentary*. Edited by Charles F. Pfeiffer and Everett F. Harrison. Chicago: Moody Press, 1963.

Lenski, R. C. H. *The Interpretation of St. Paul's First and Second Epistle to the Corinthians*. Columbus, OH: Wartburg Press, 1946.

Morgan, G. Campbell. *The Corinthian Letters of Paul*. Old Tappan, NJ: Fleming H. Revell Co., 1946.

Morris, Leon. *The First Epistle of Paul to the Corinthians*. Grand Rapids: Wm. B. Eerdmans Publishing Co., 1975.

Robertson, Archibald Thomas. *Word Pictures in the New Testament*, vol. 4. Nashville, TN: Broadman Press, 1931.

Robertson, Archibald and Plummer, Alfred. *A Critical and Exegetical Commentary on the First Epistle of St. Paul to the Corinthians*. Edinburgh: T. & T. Clark, 1955.